MW01617841

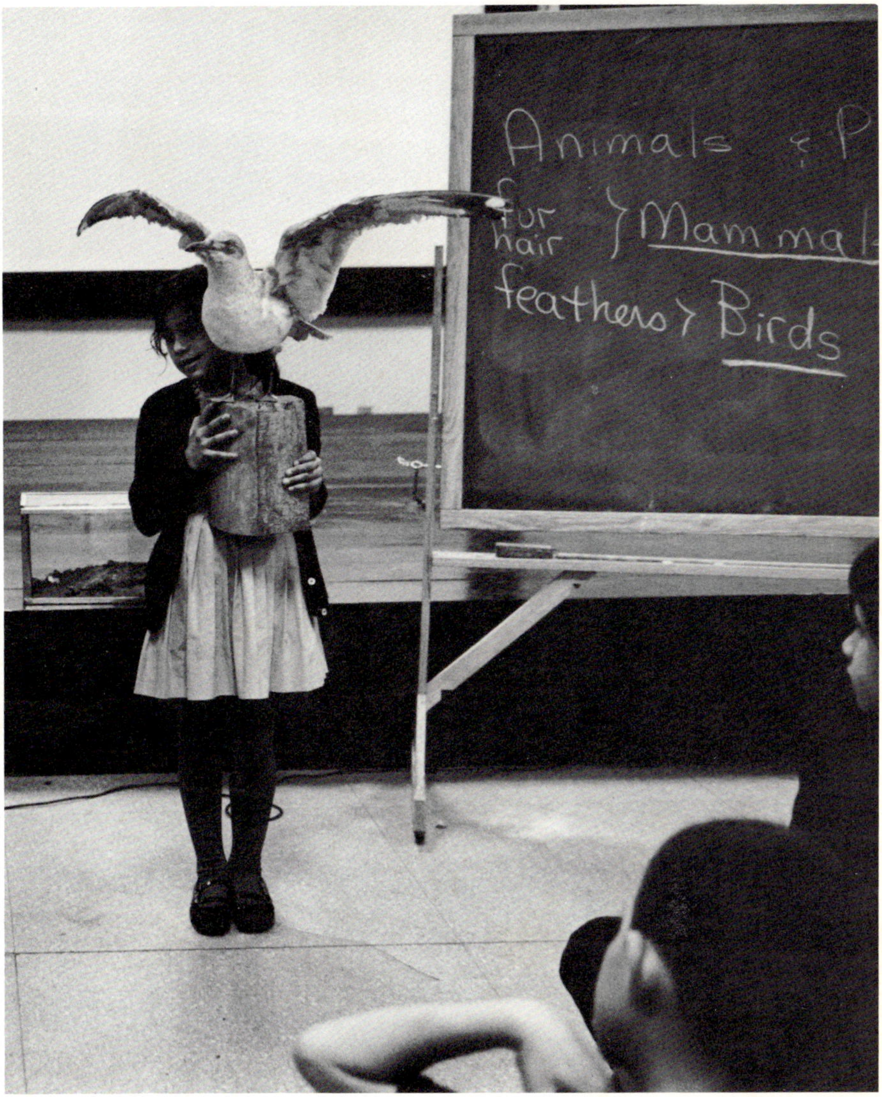

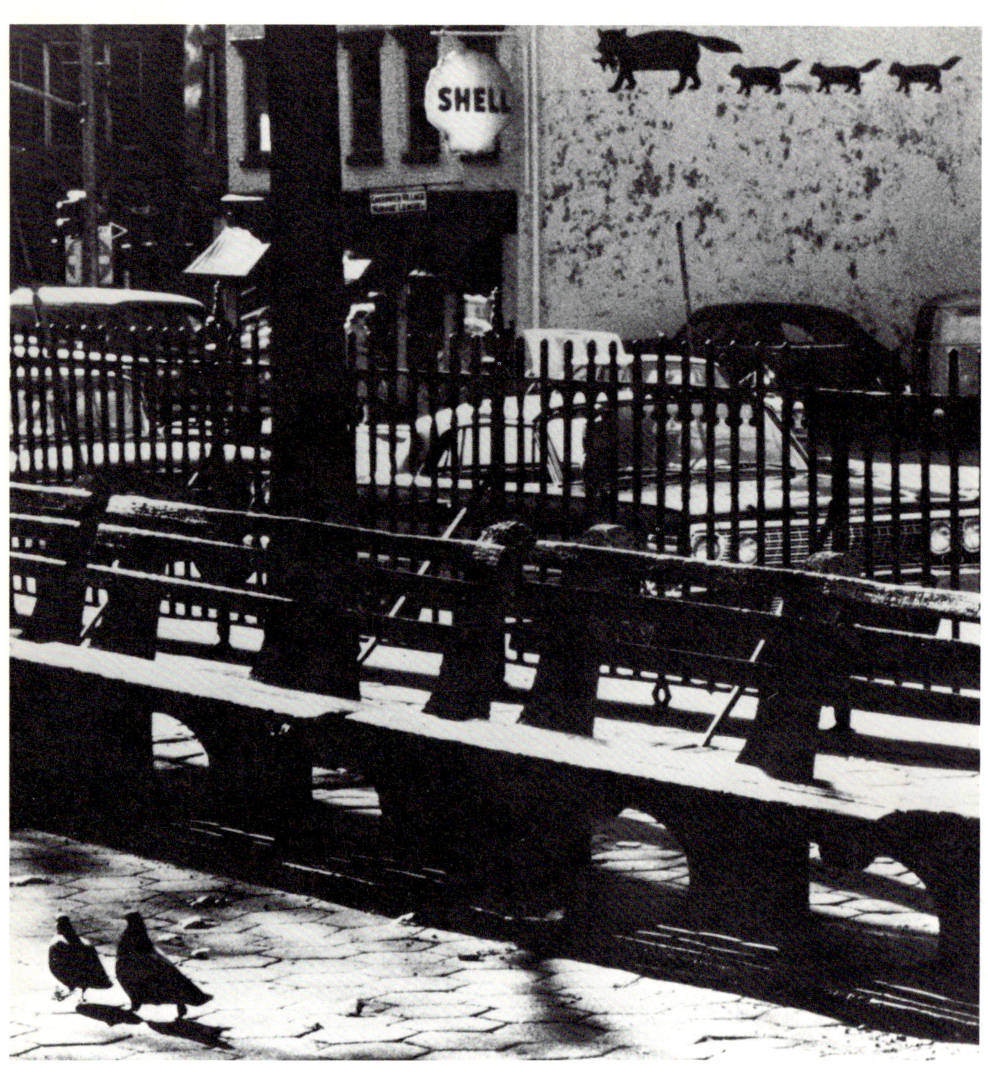
SHELL

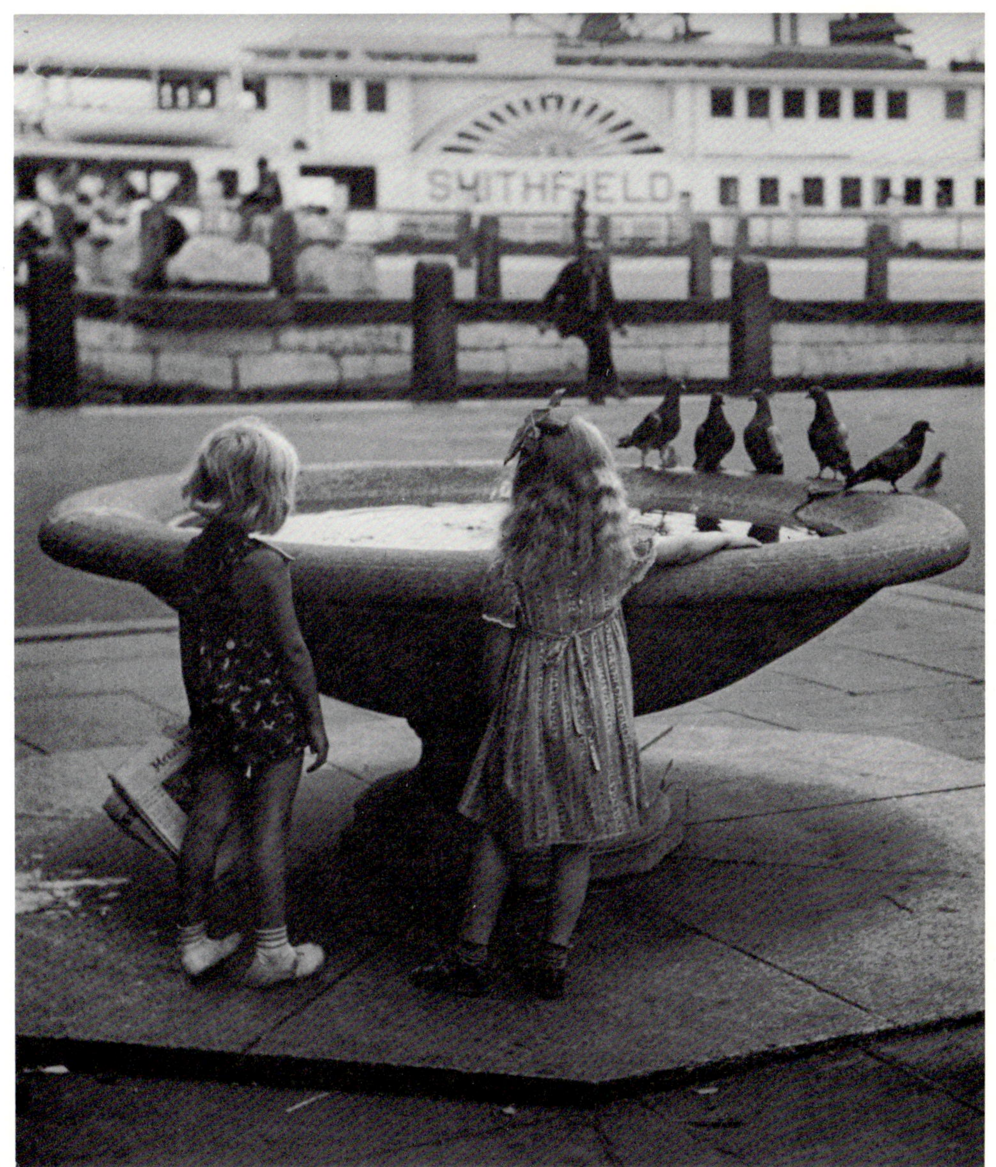
SMITHFIELD

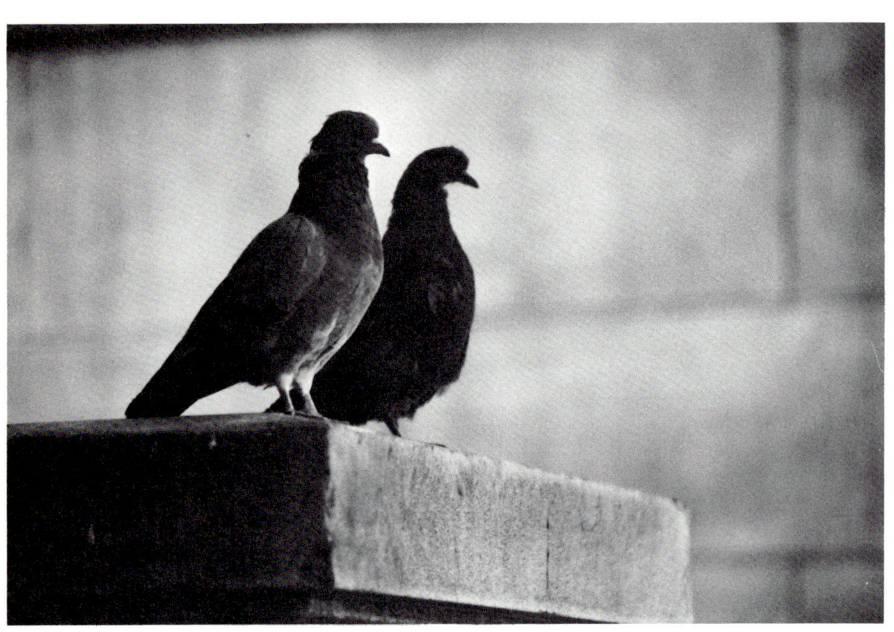

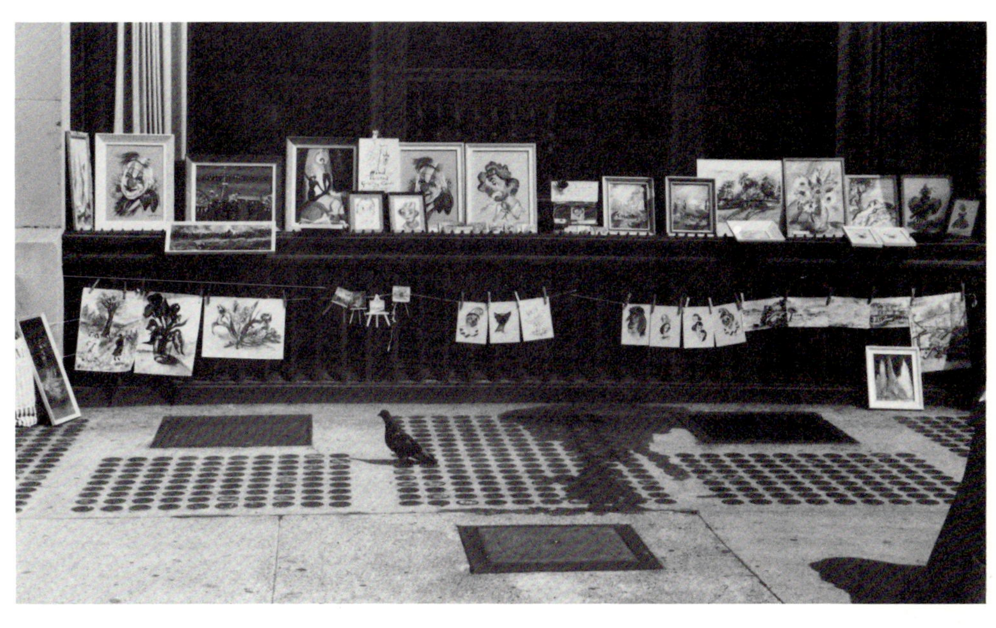

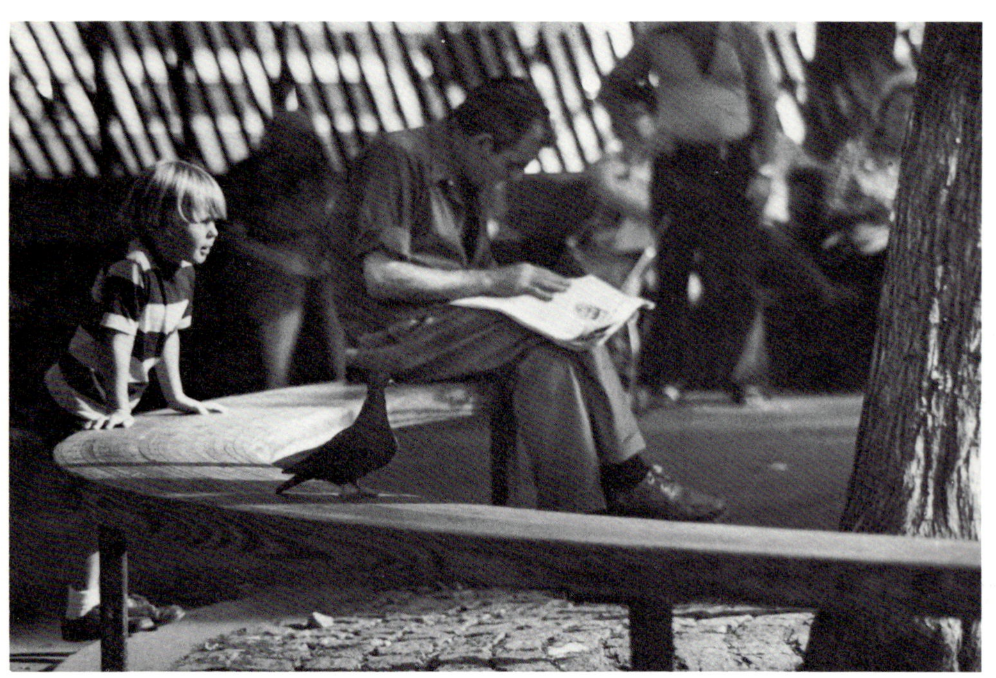

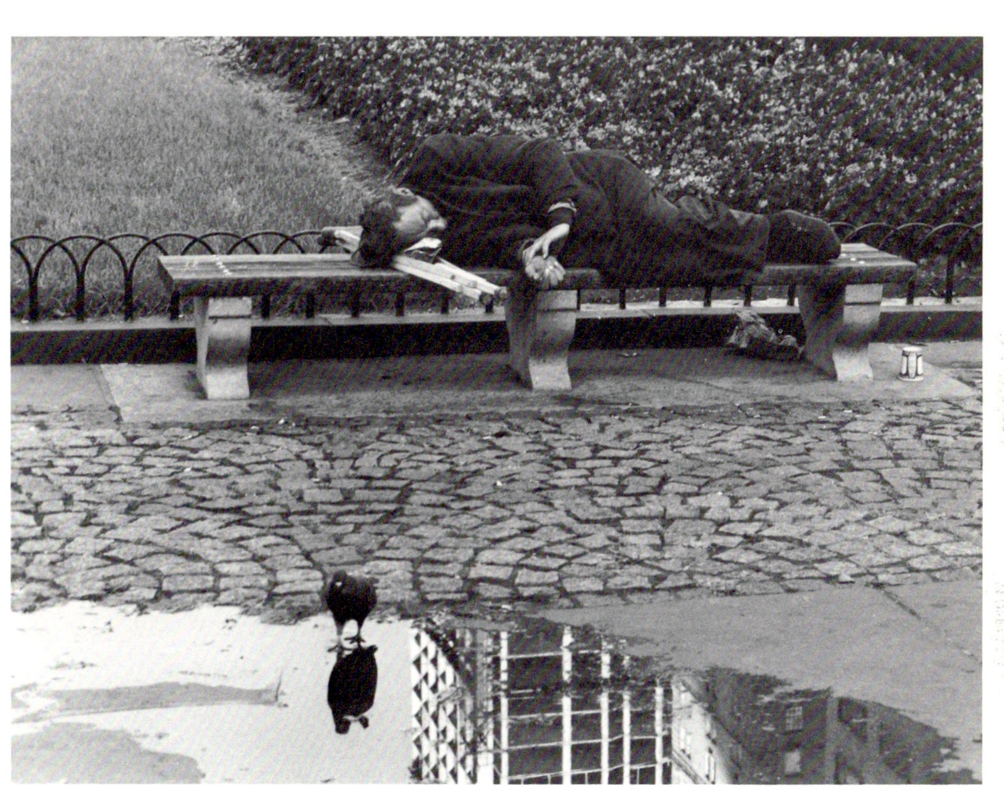

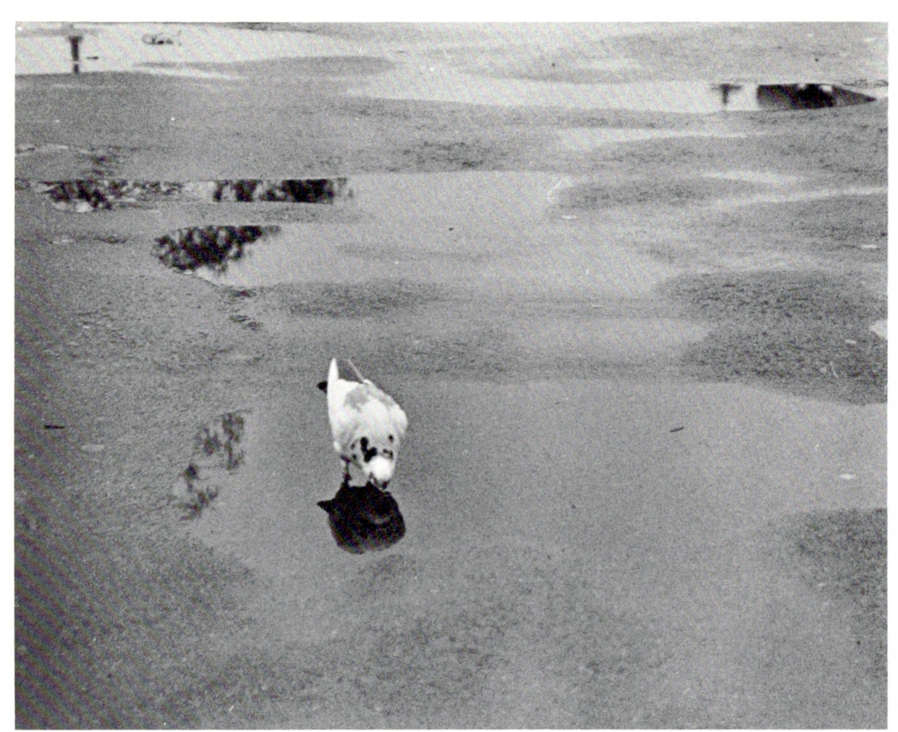

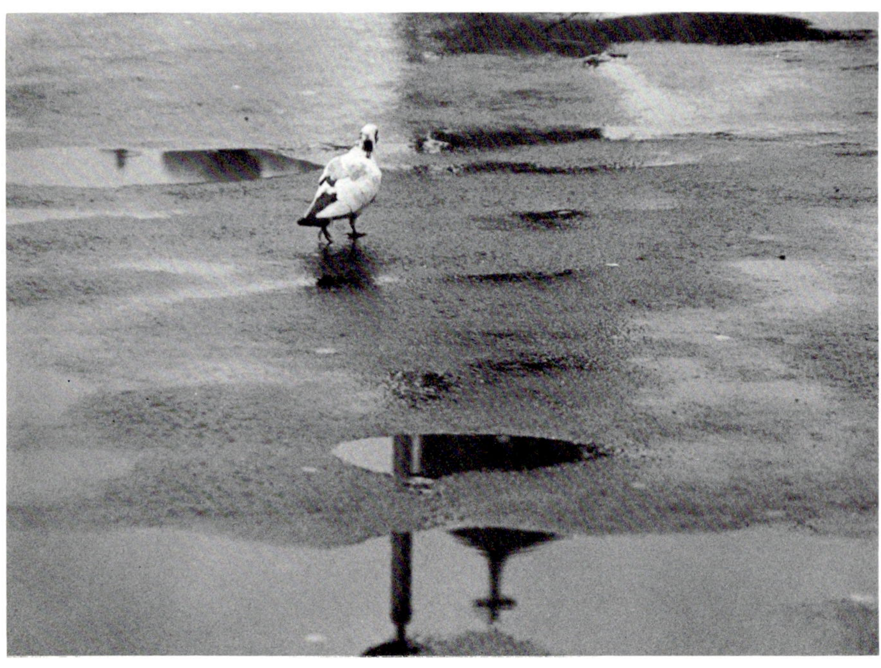

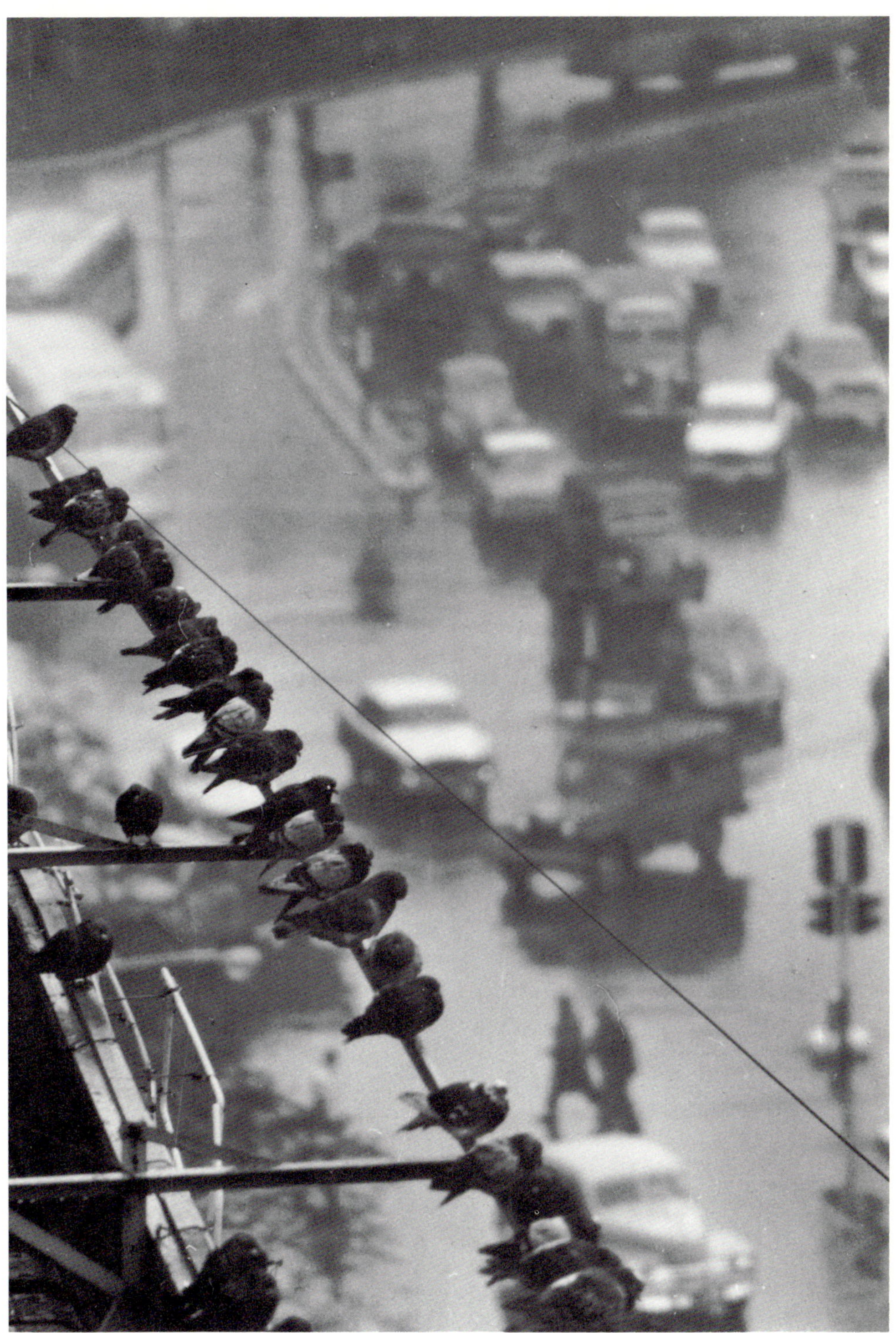

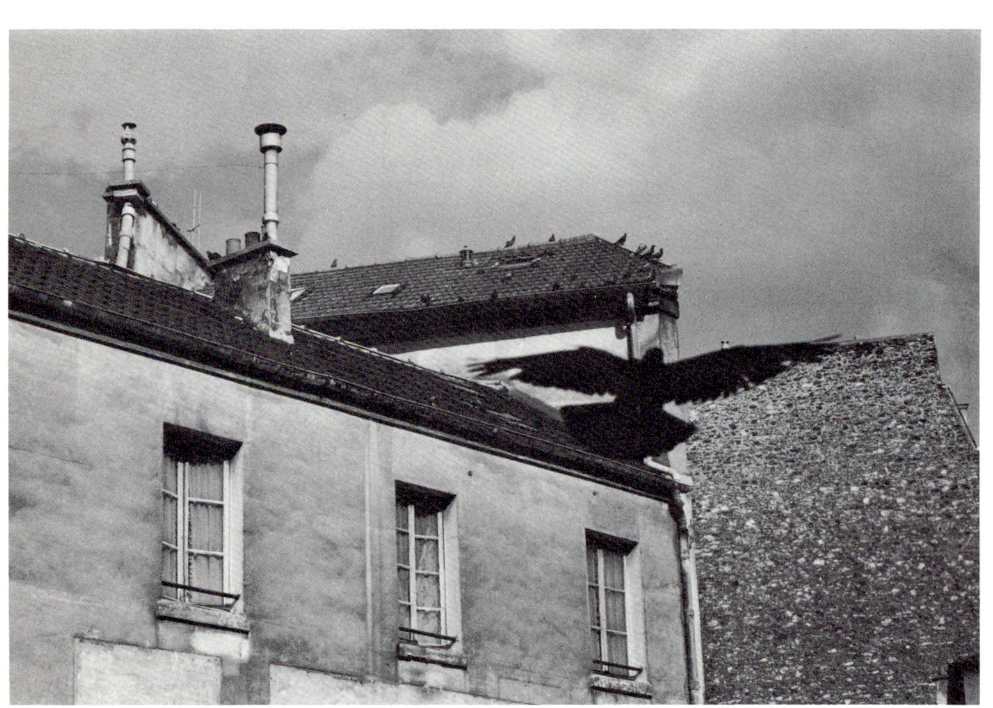

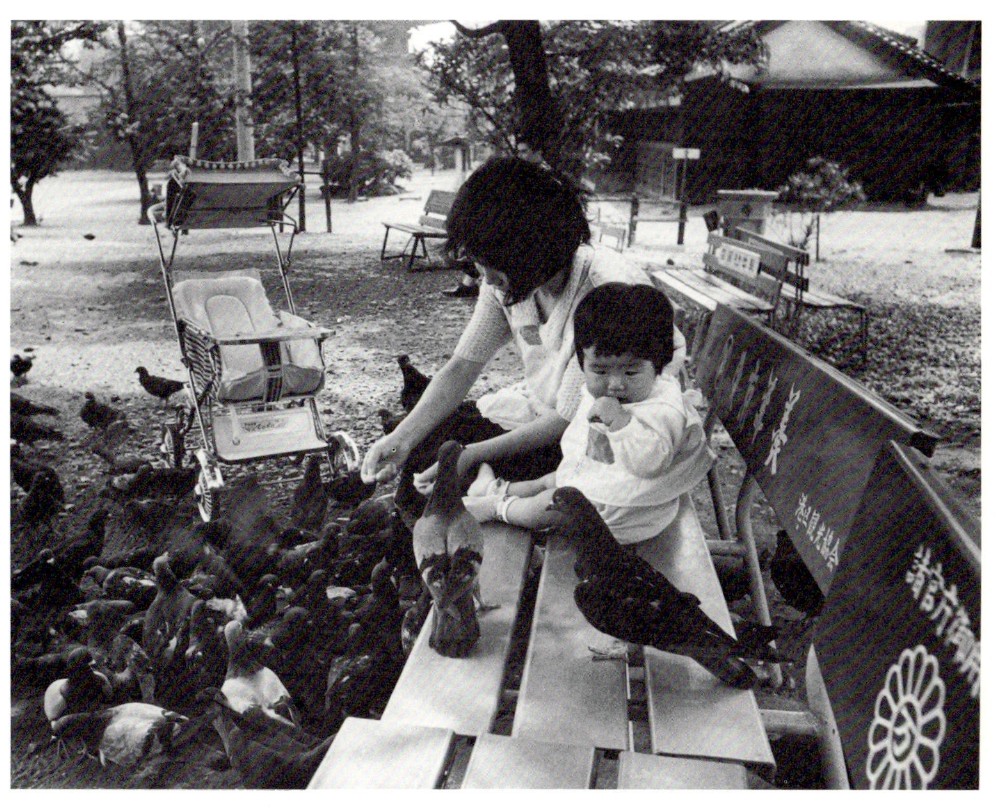

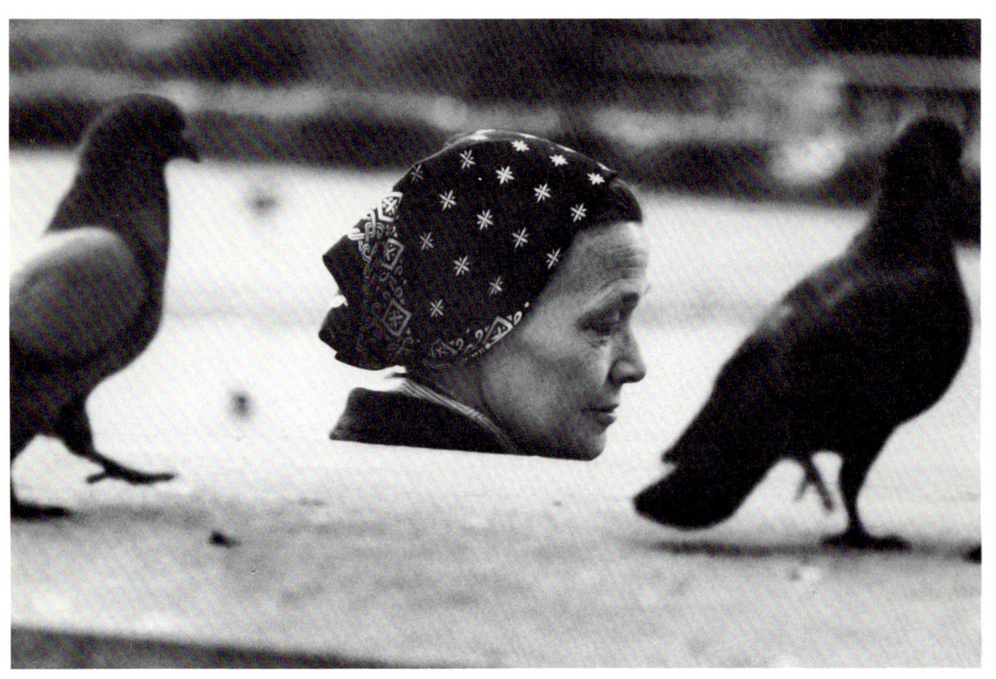

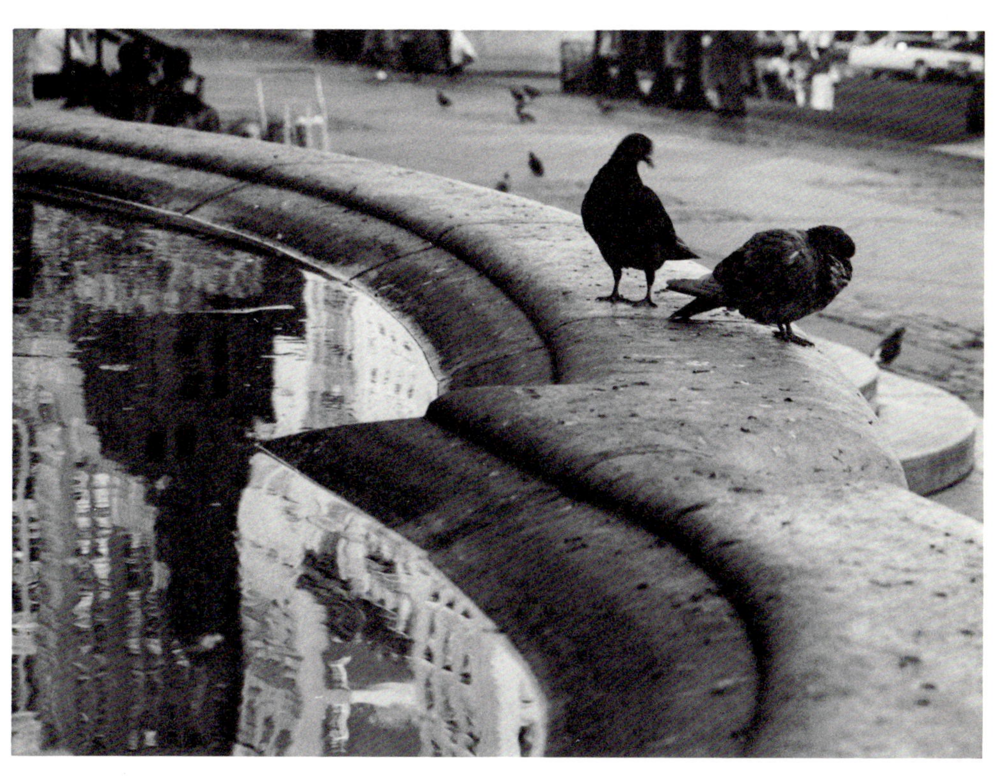

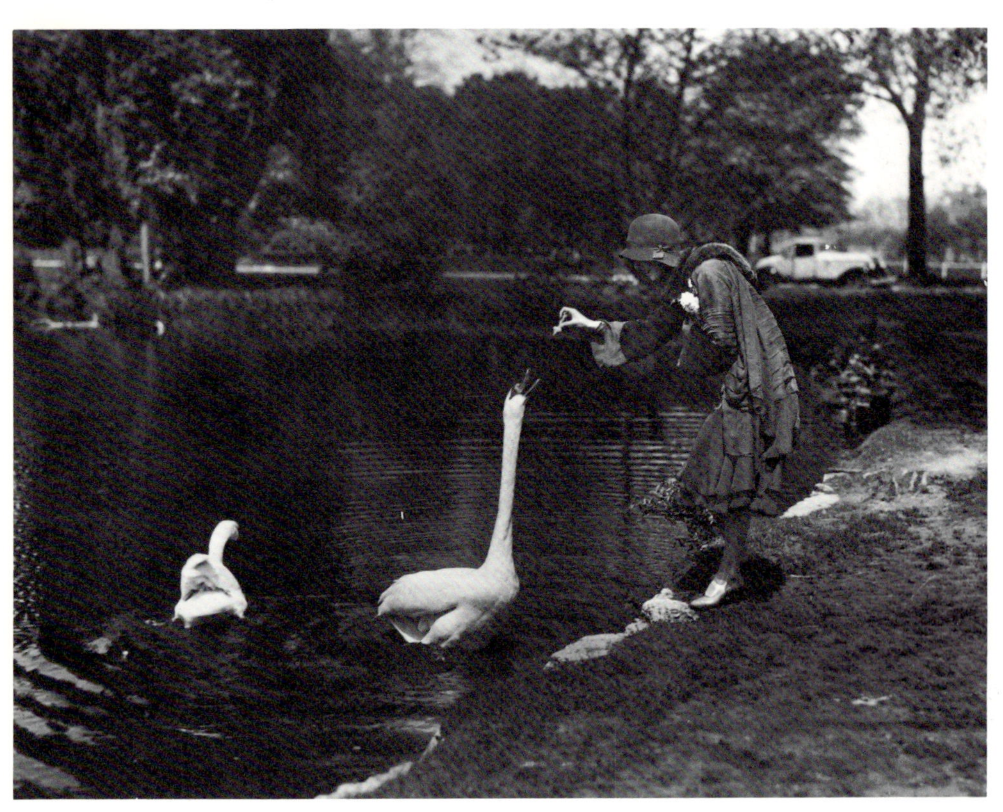

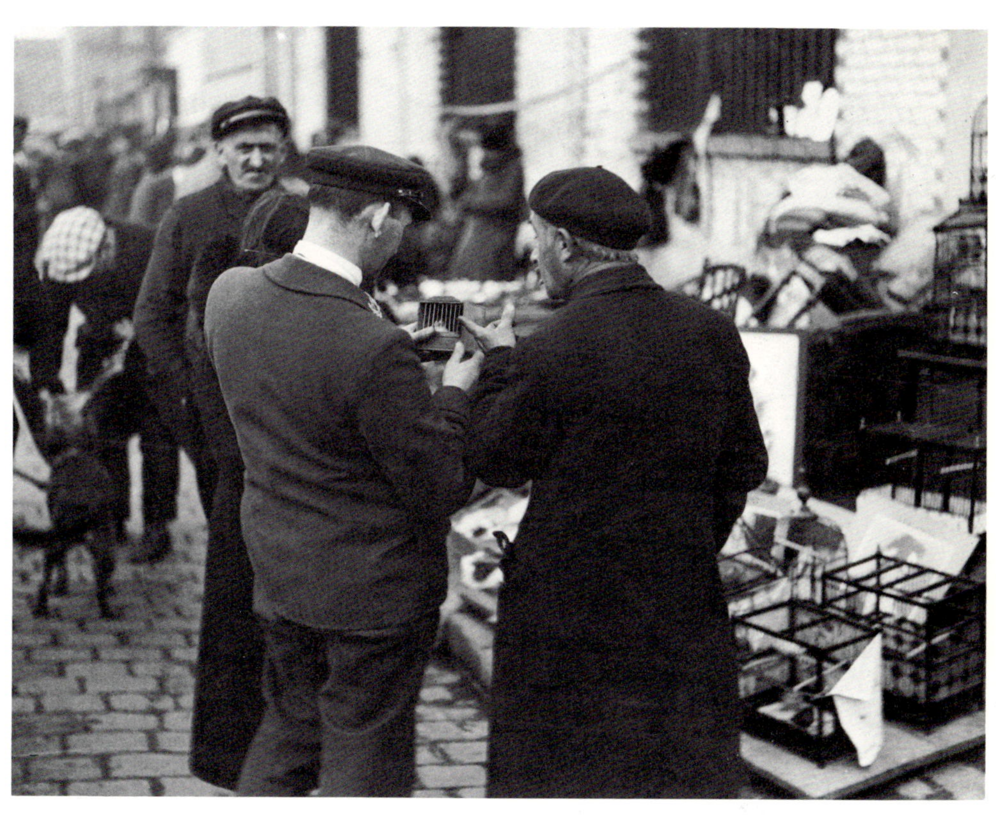

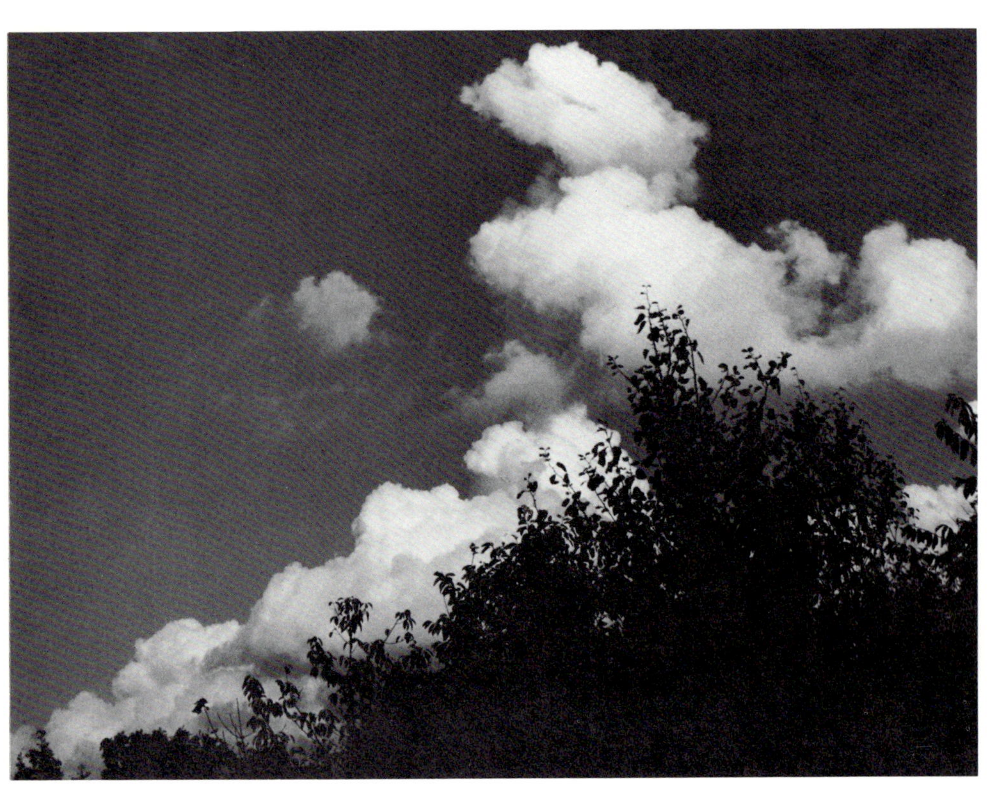

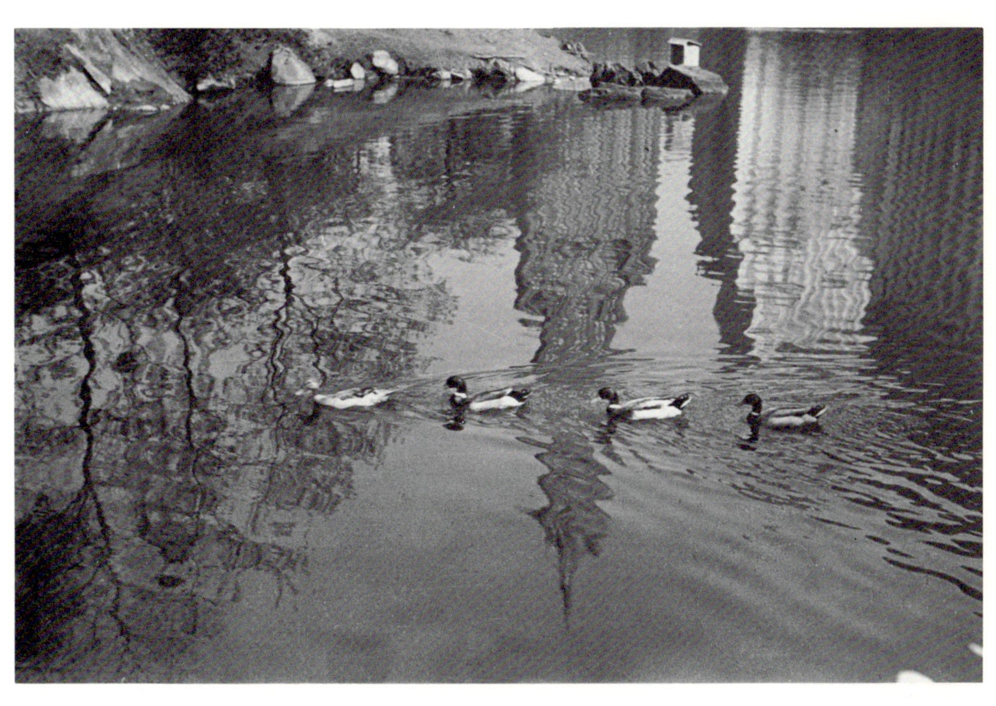

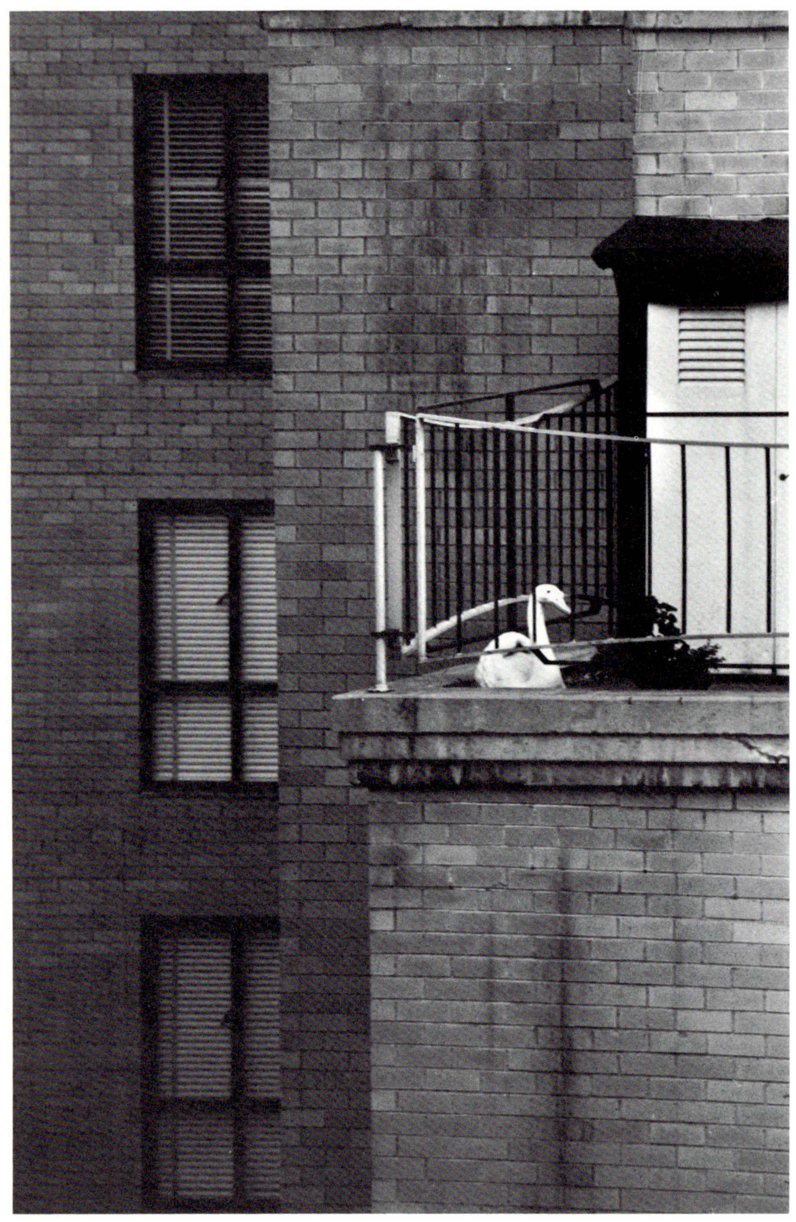

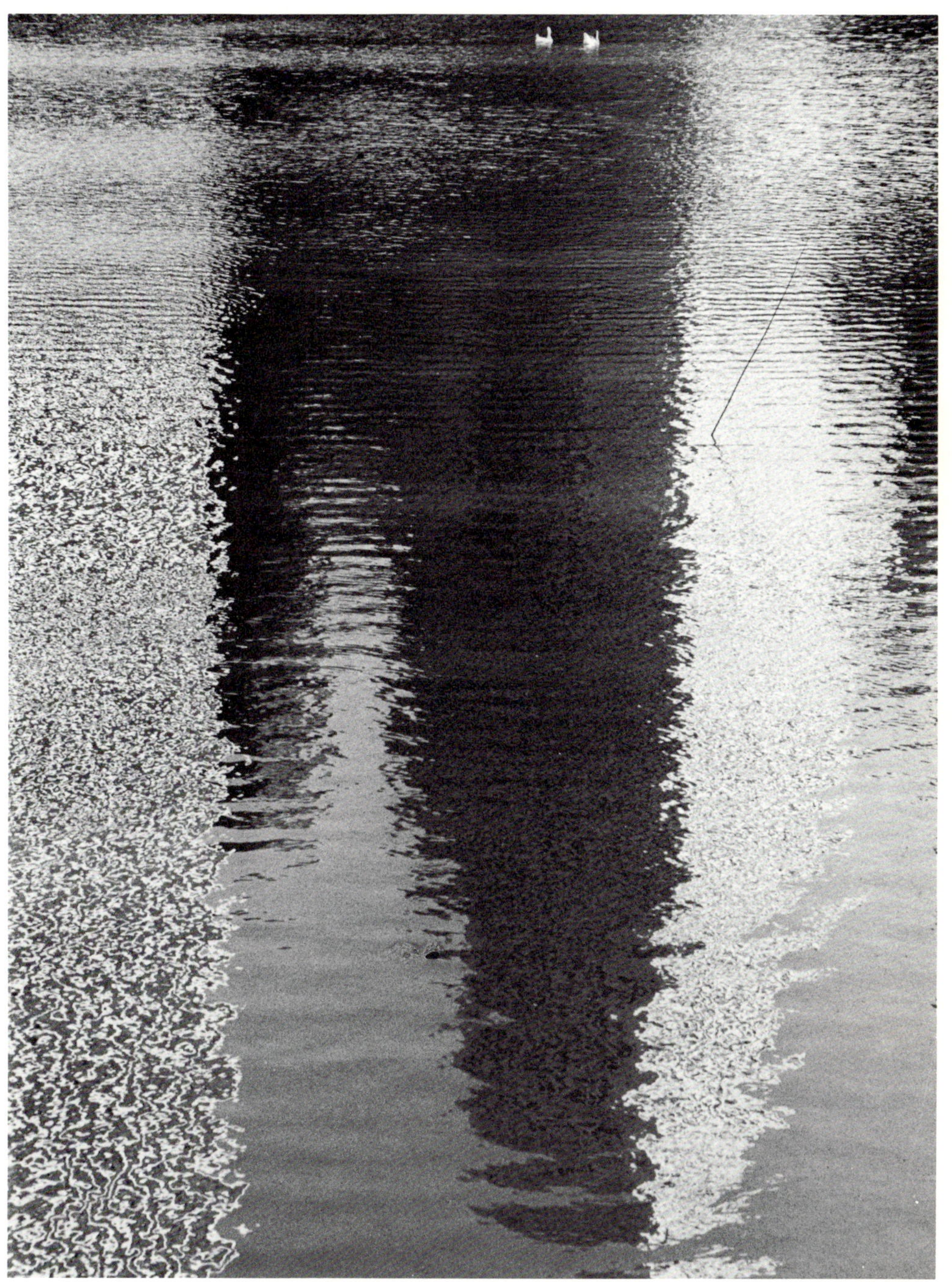

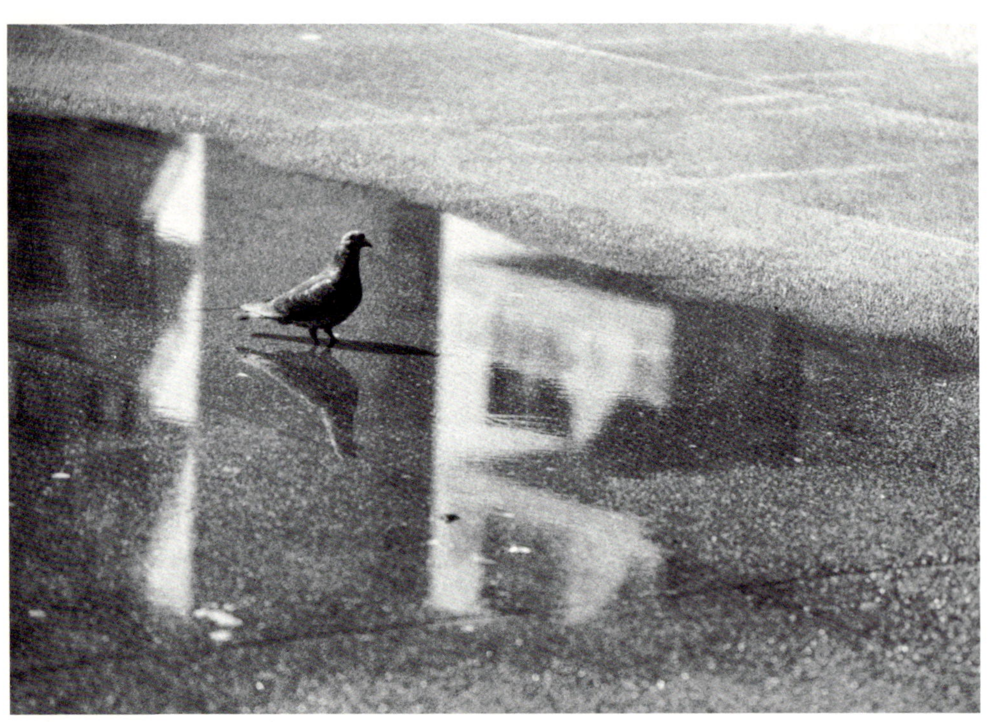

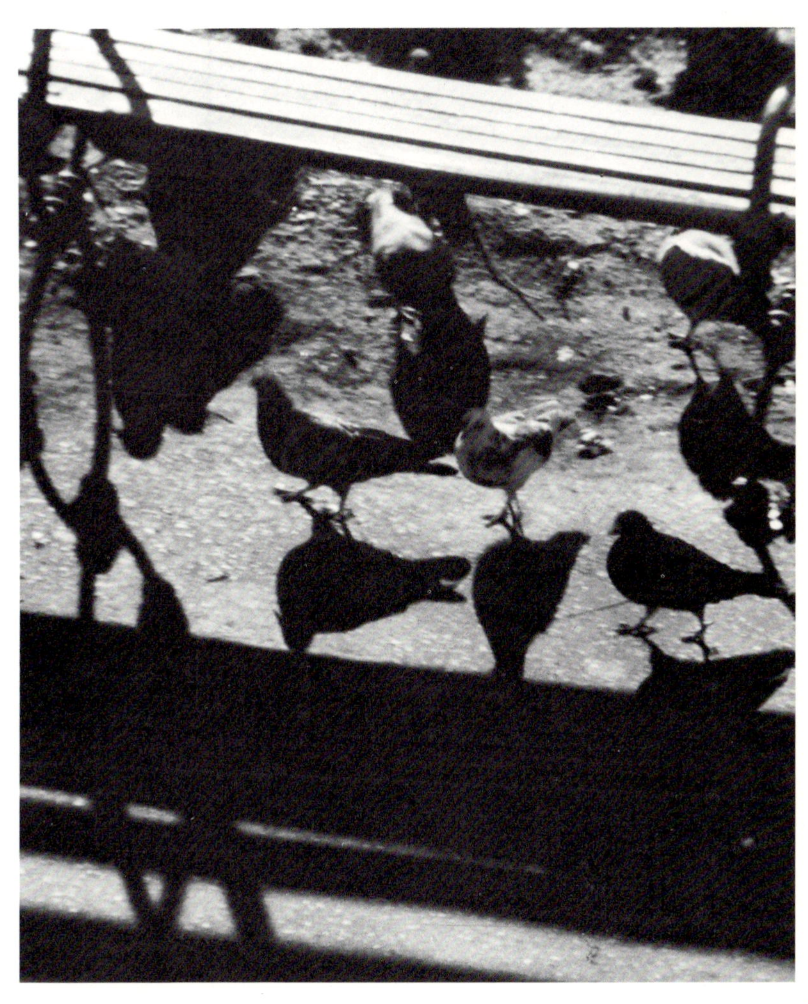

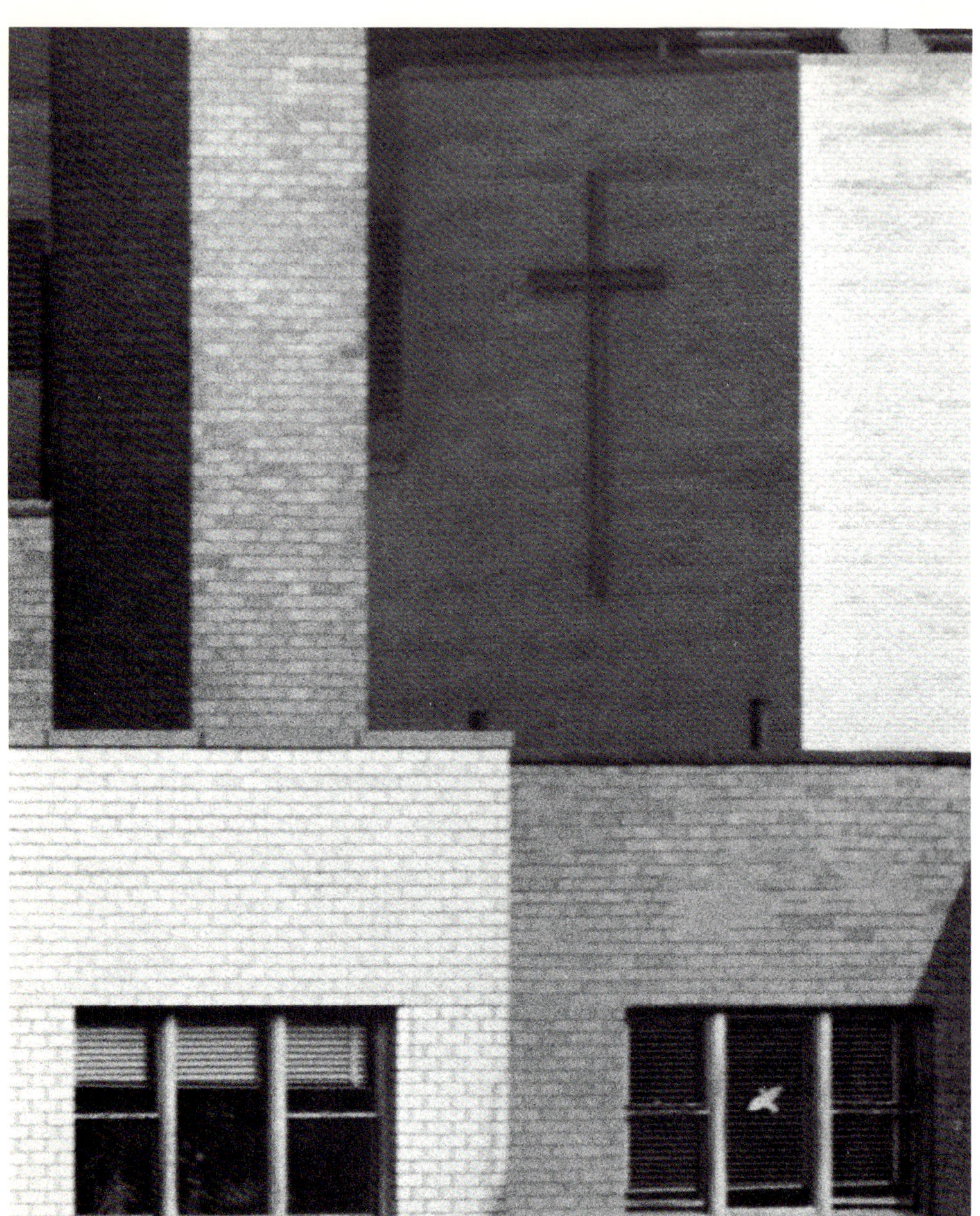

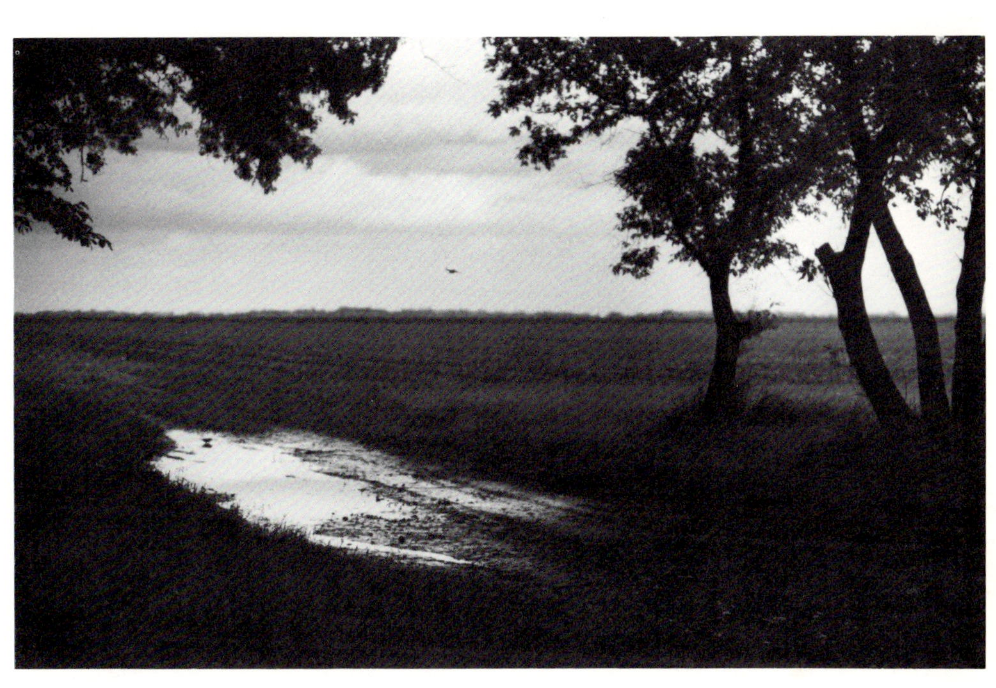

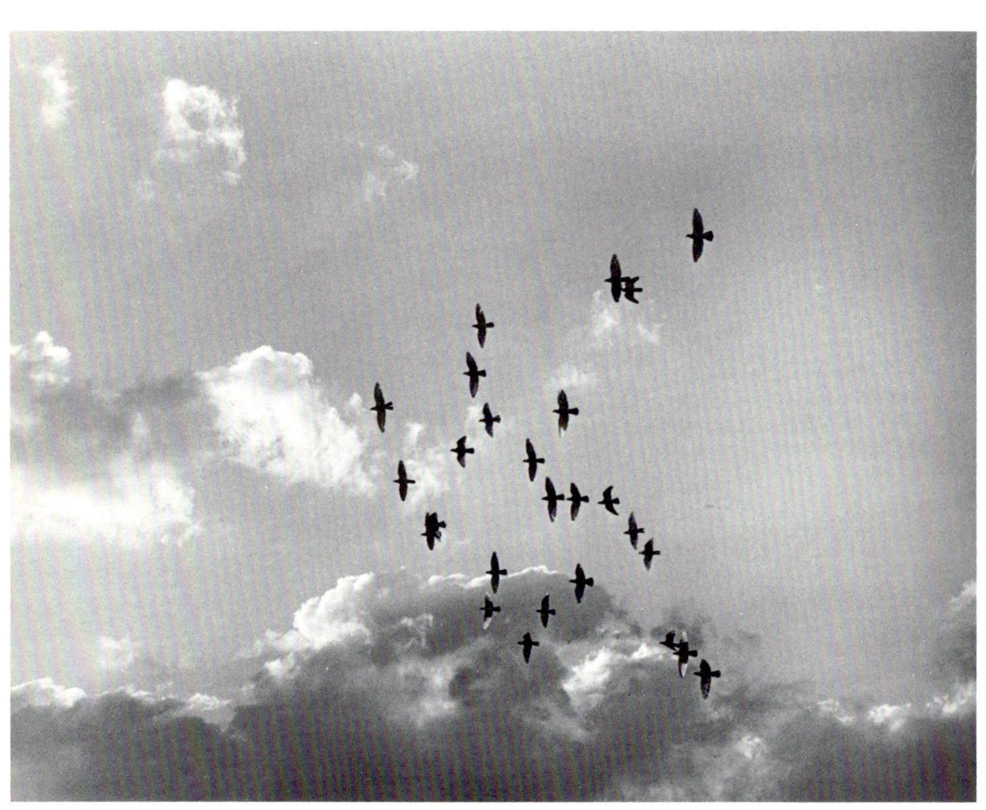

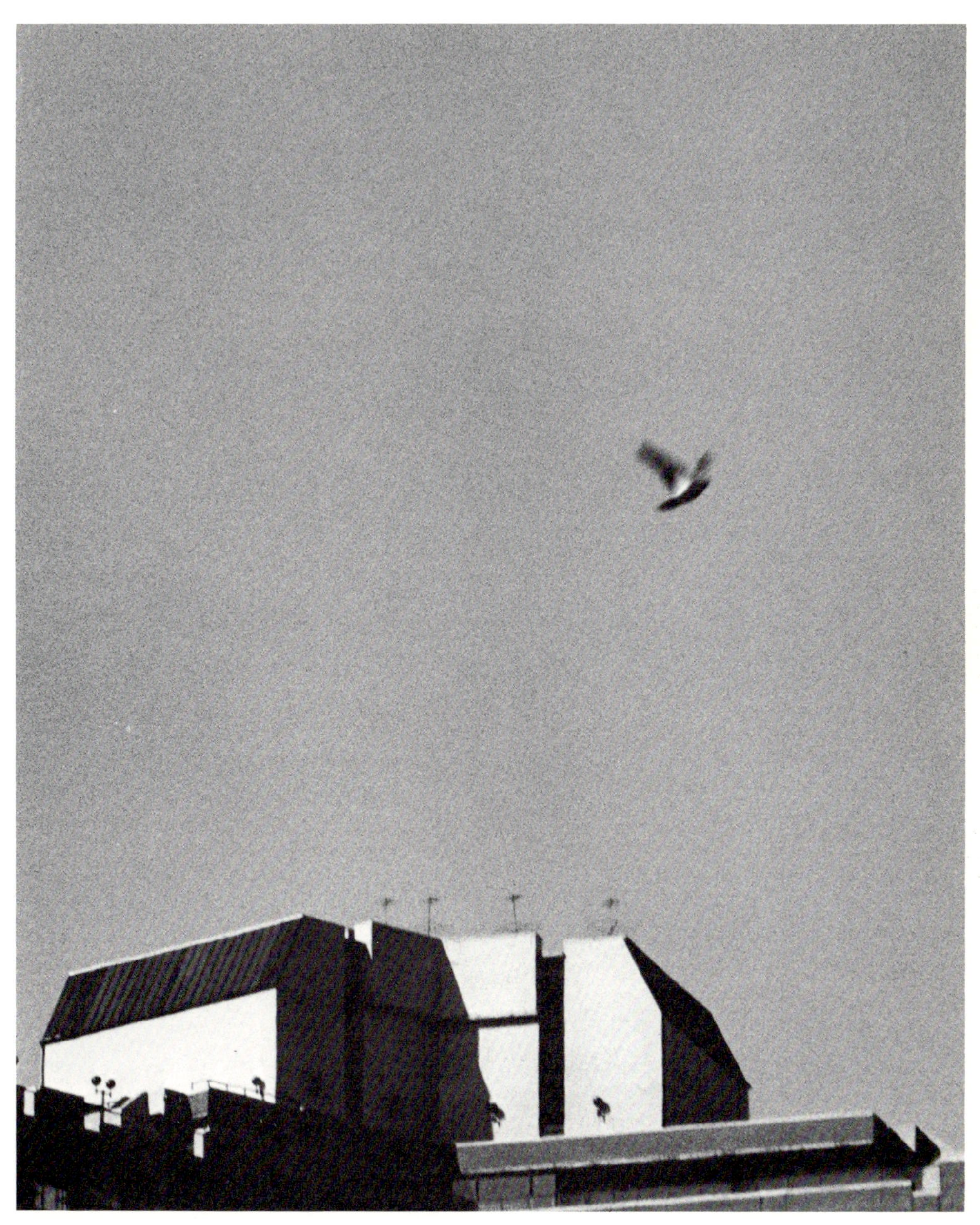

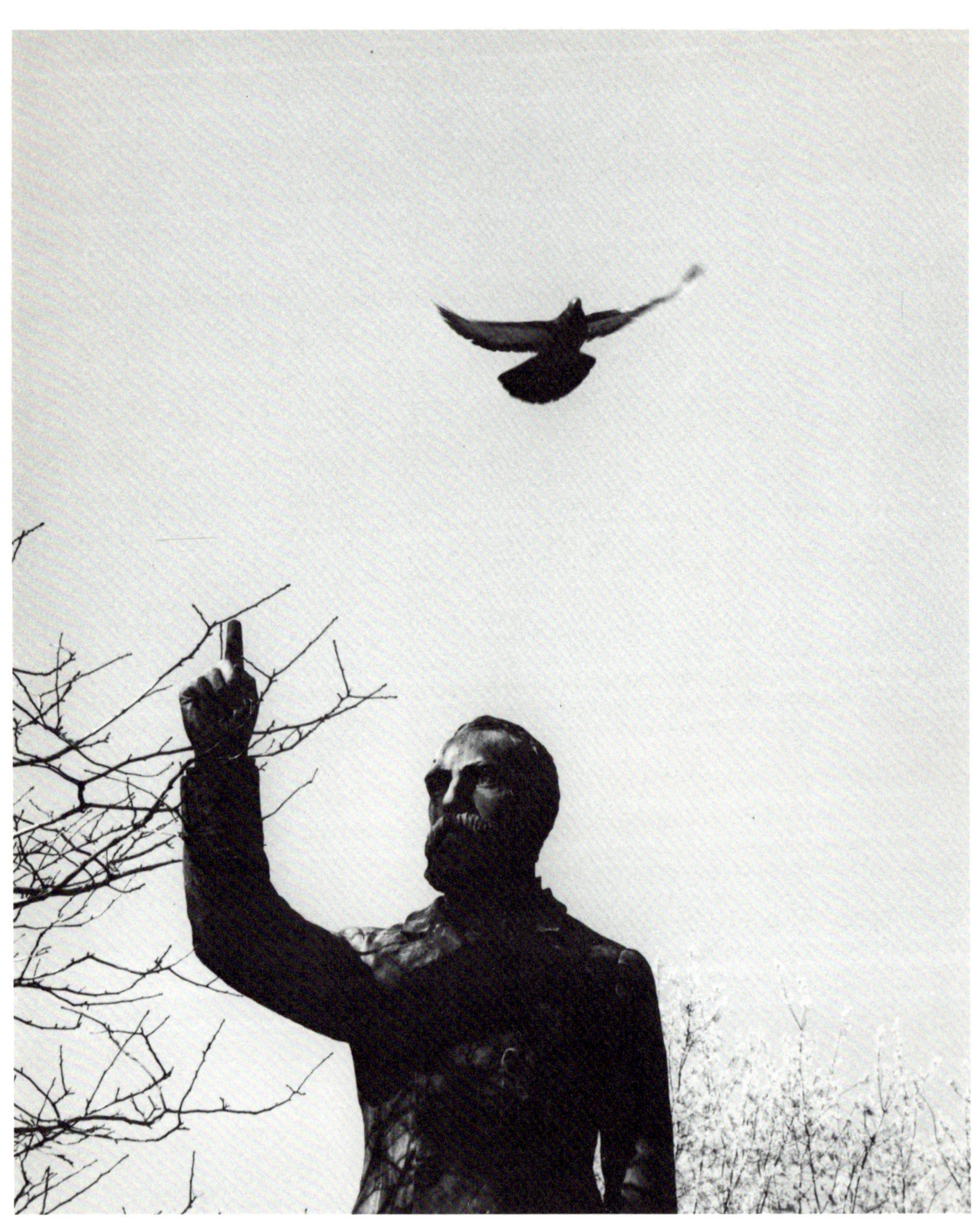

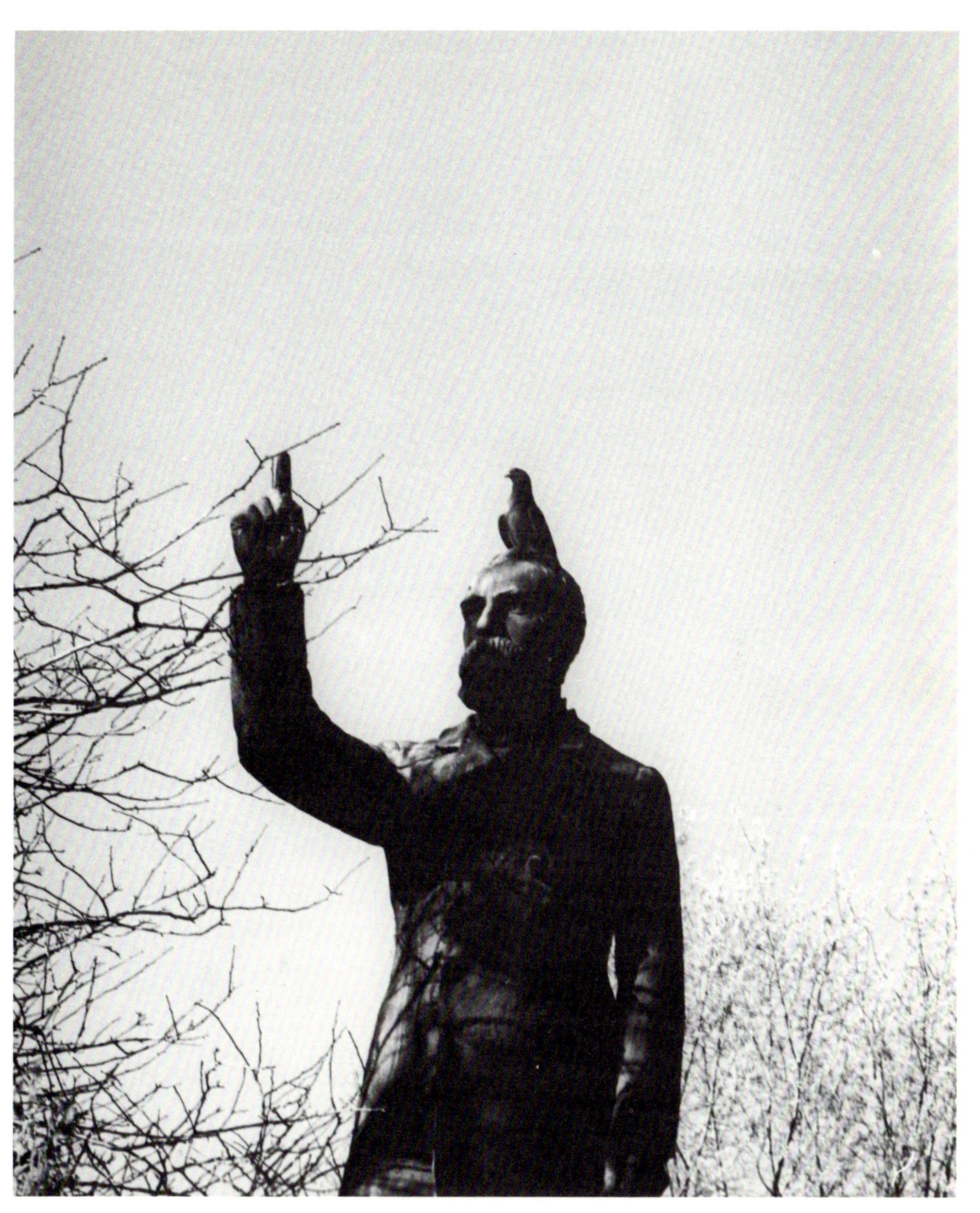

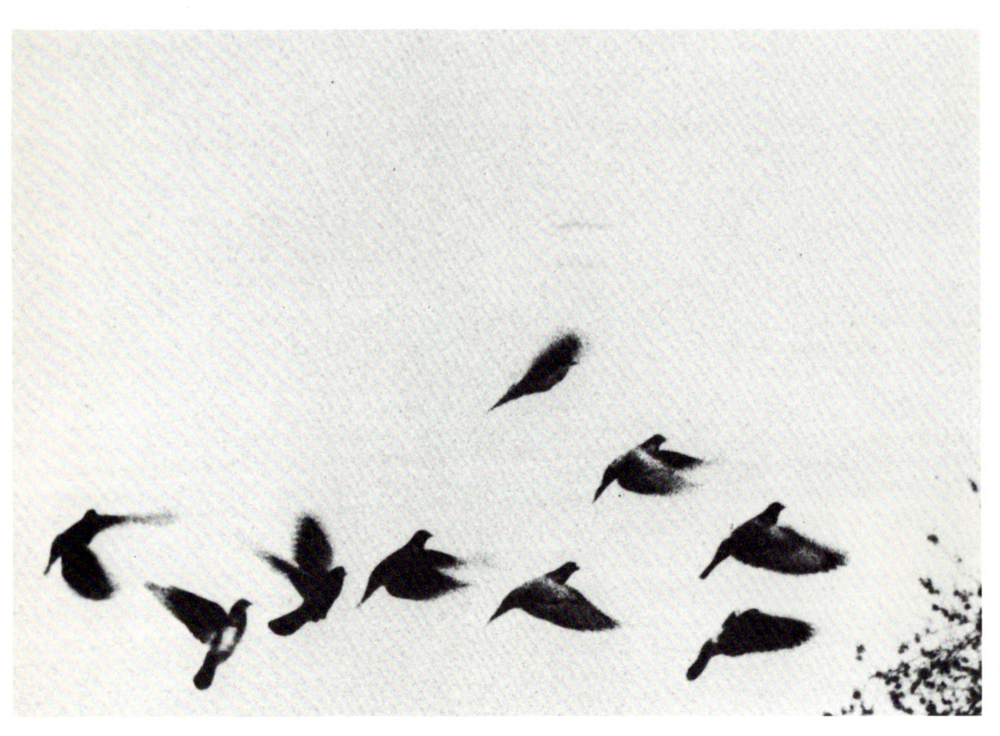

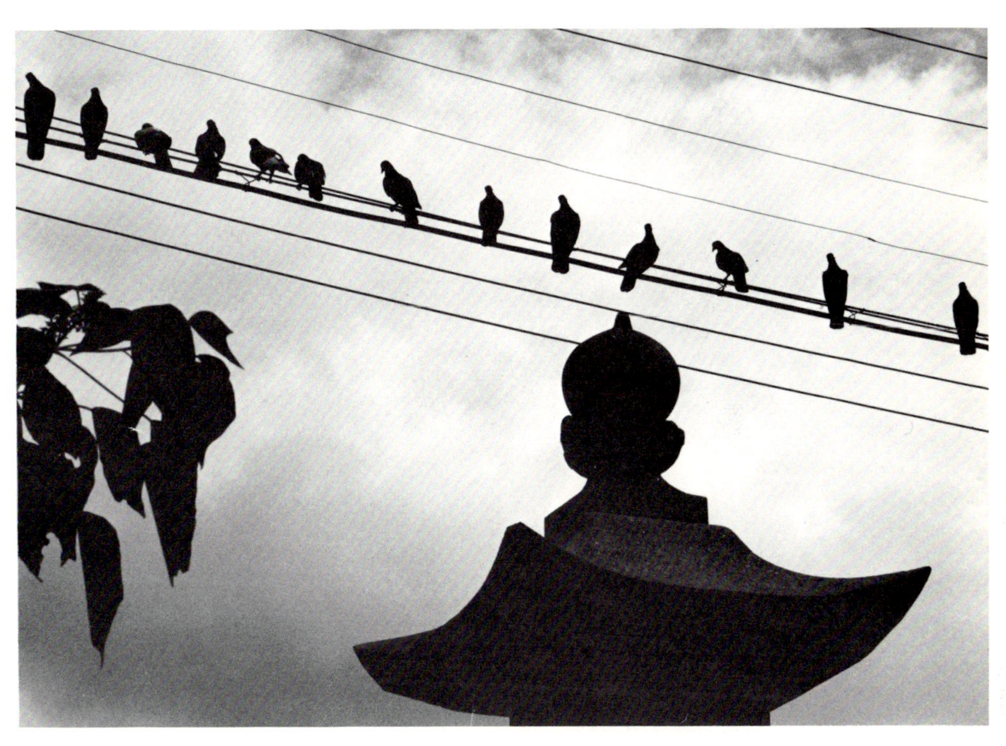

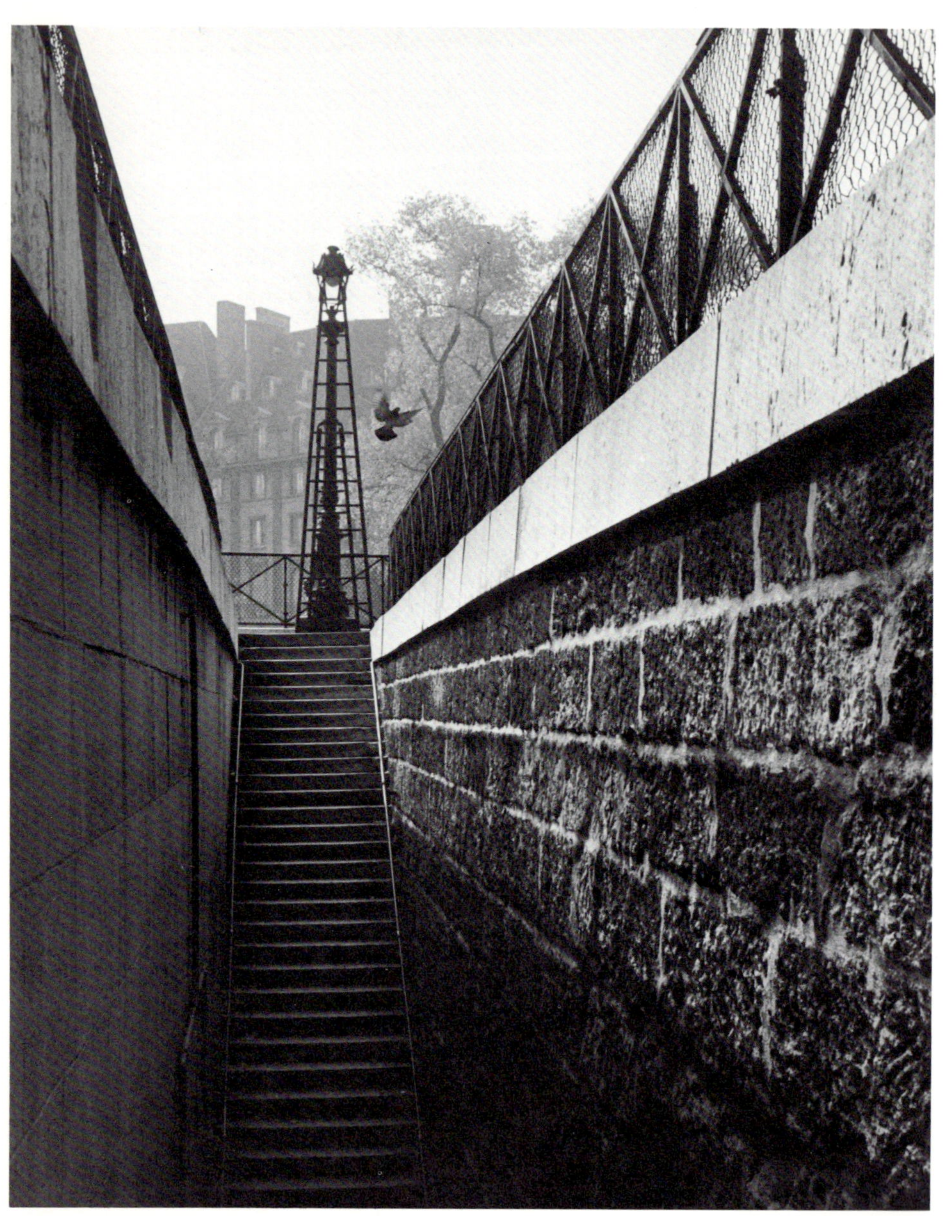

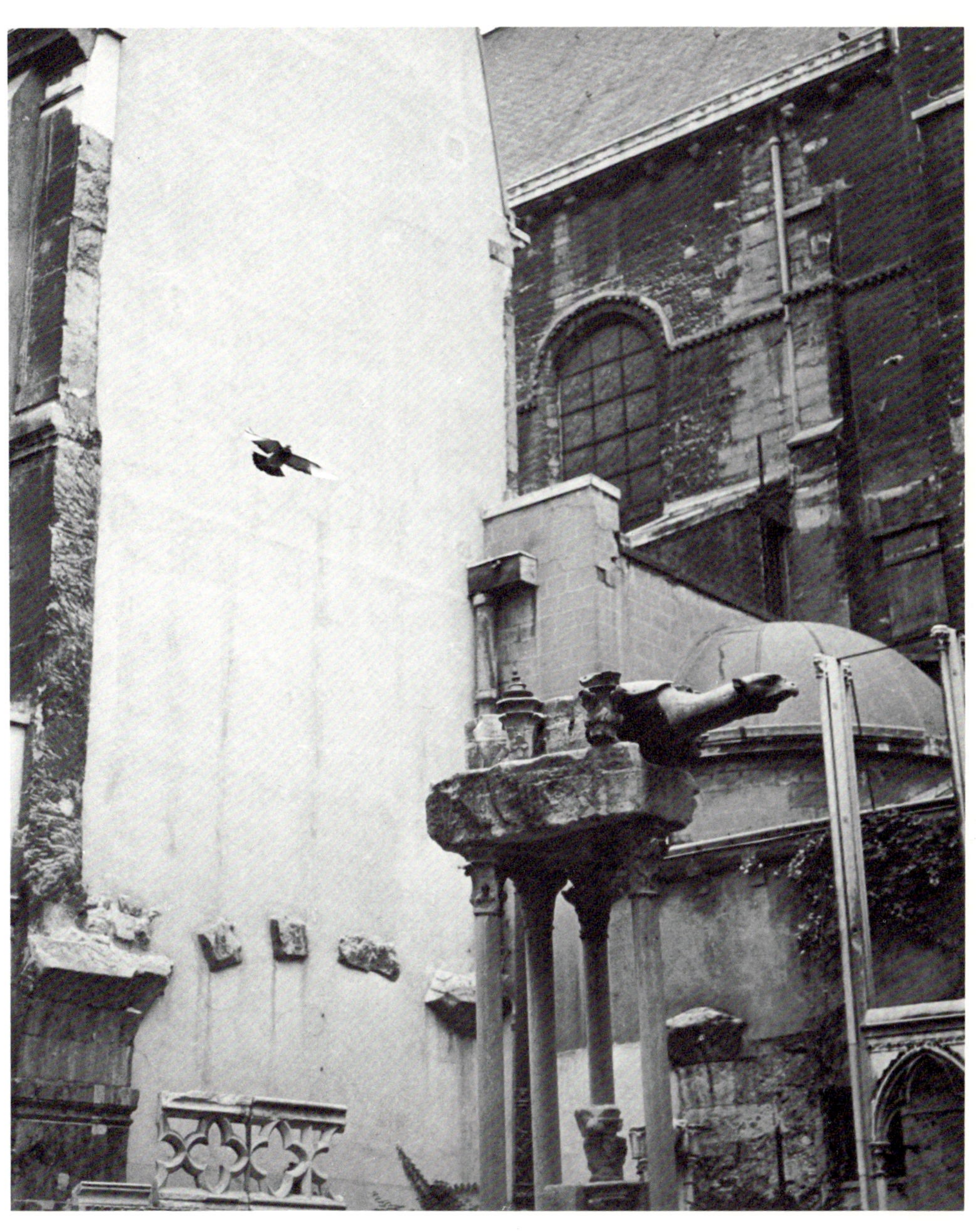

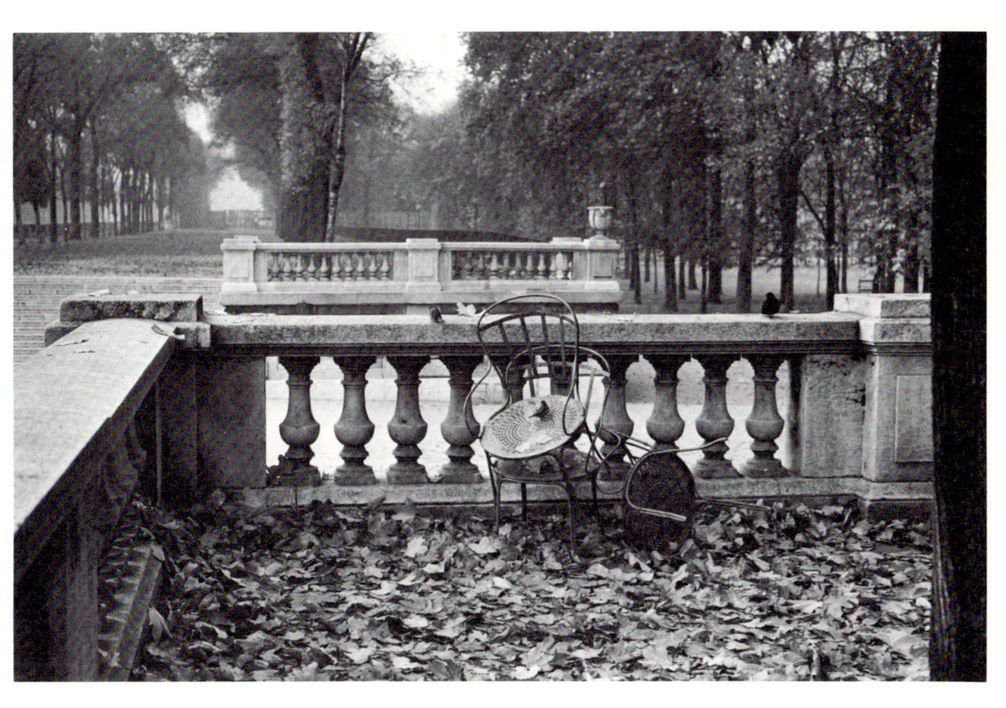

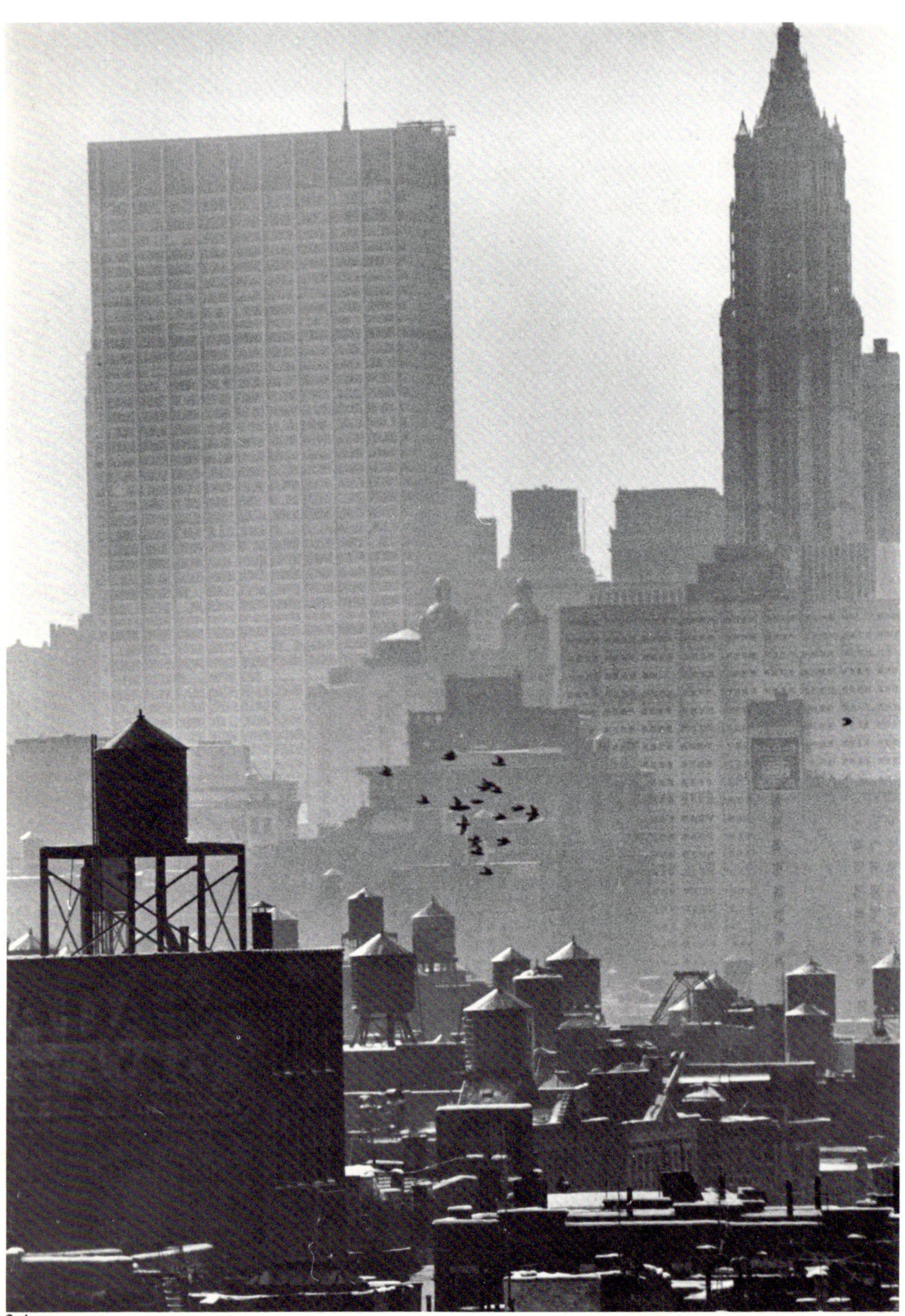

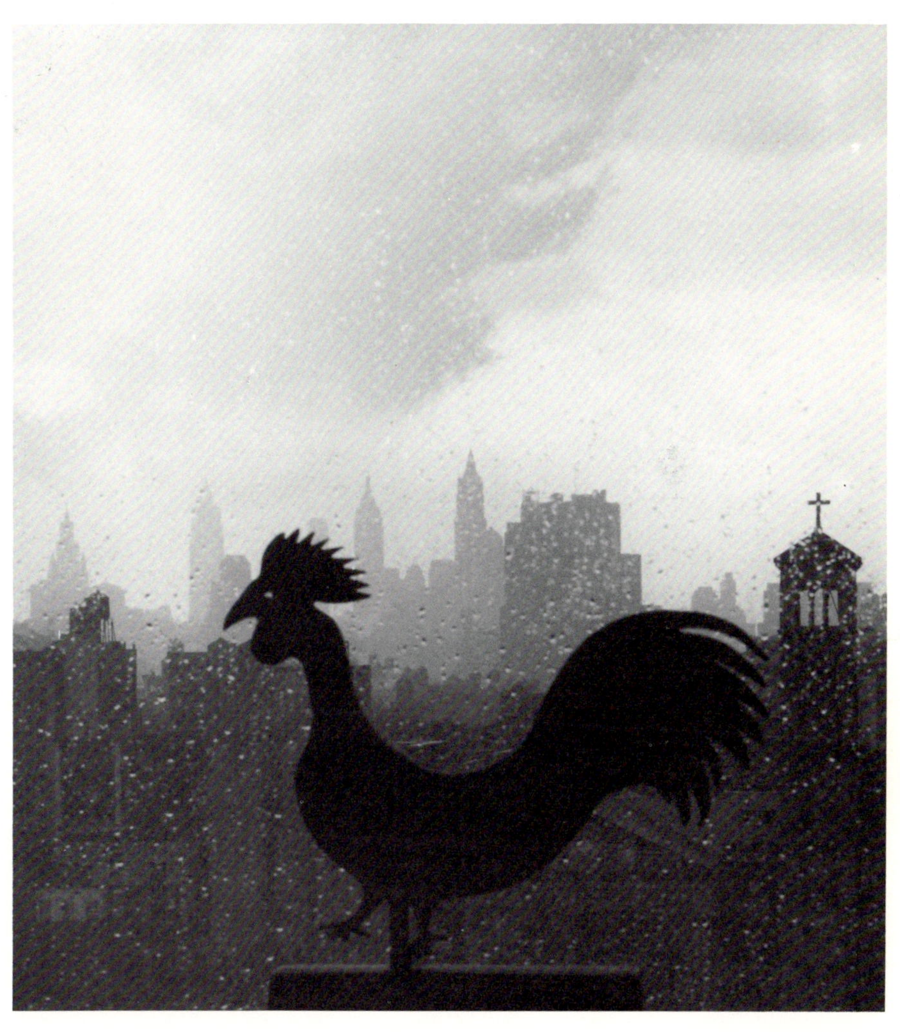

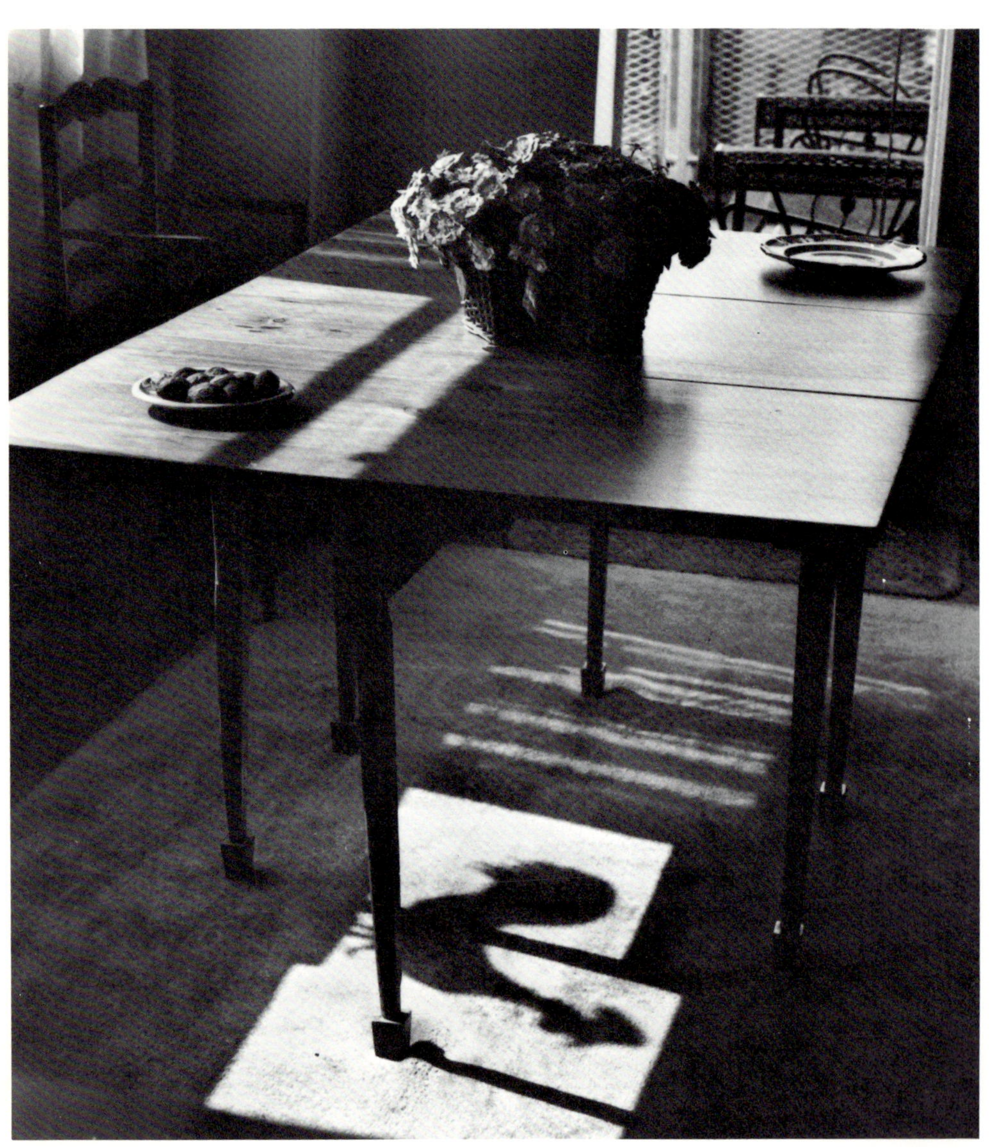

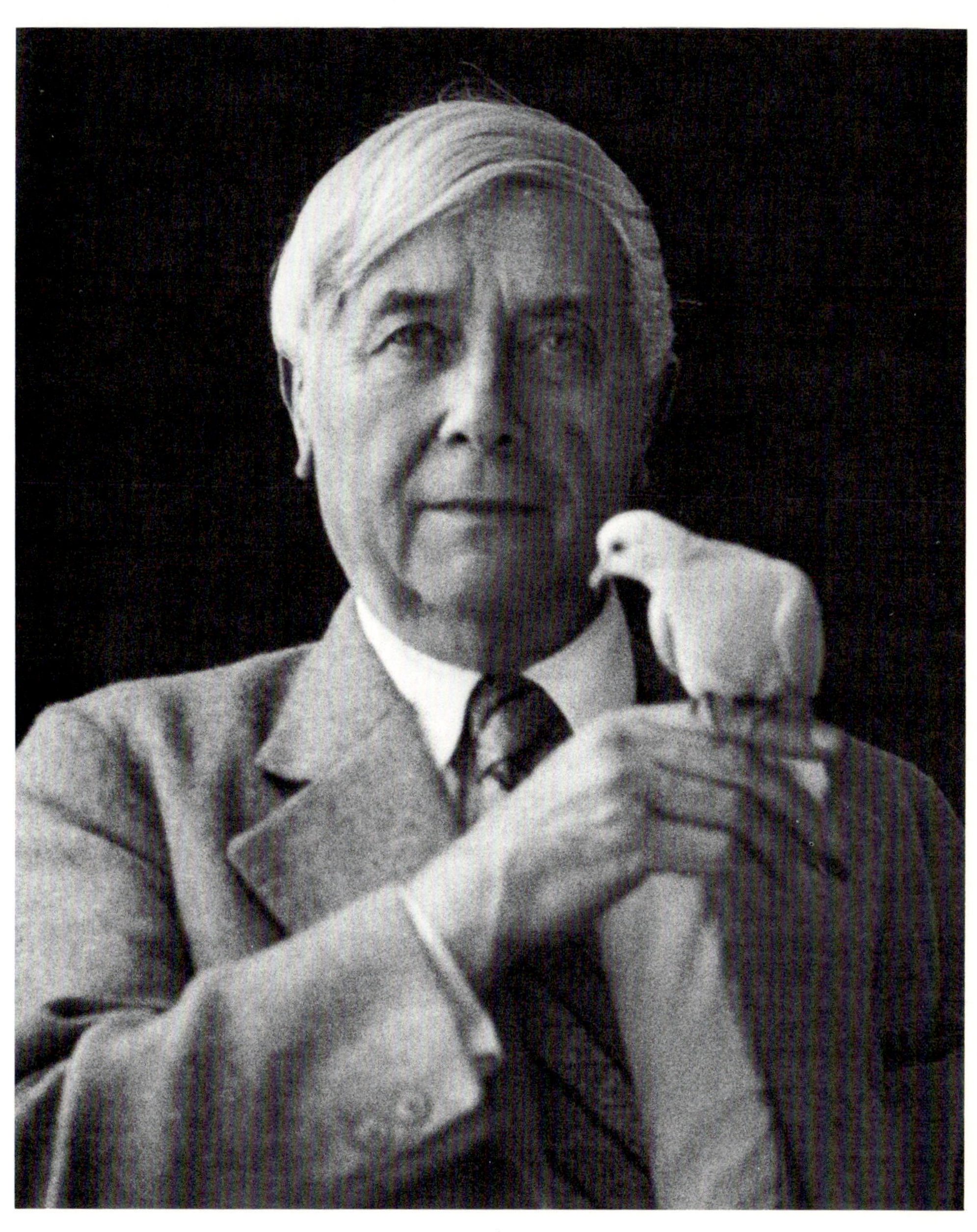

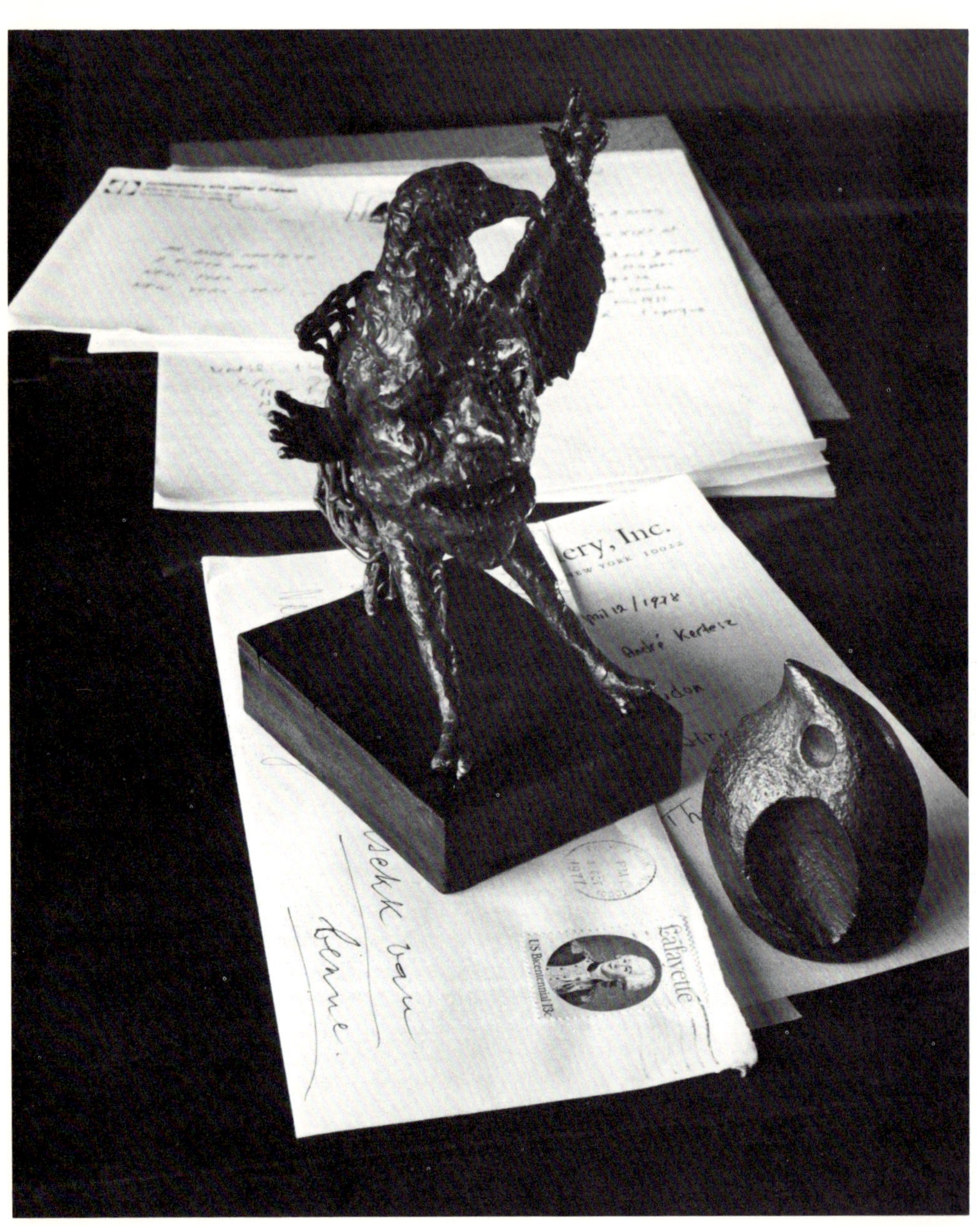
ery, Inc.
NEW YORK 10022
Lafayette
US Bicentennial 13c

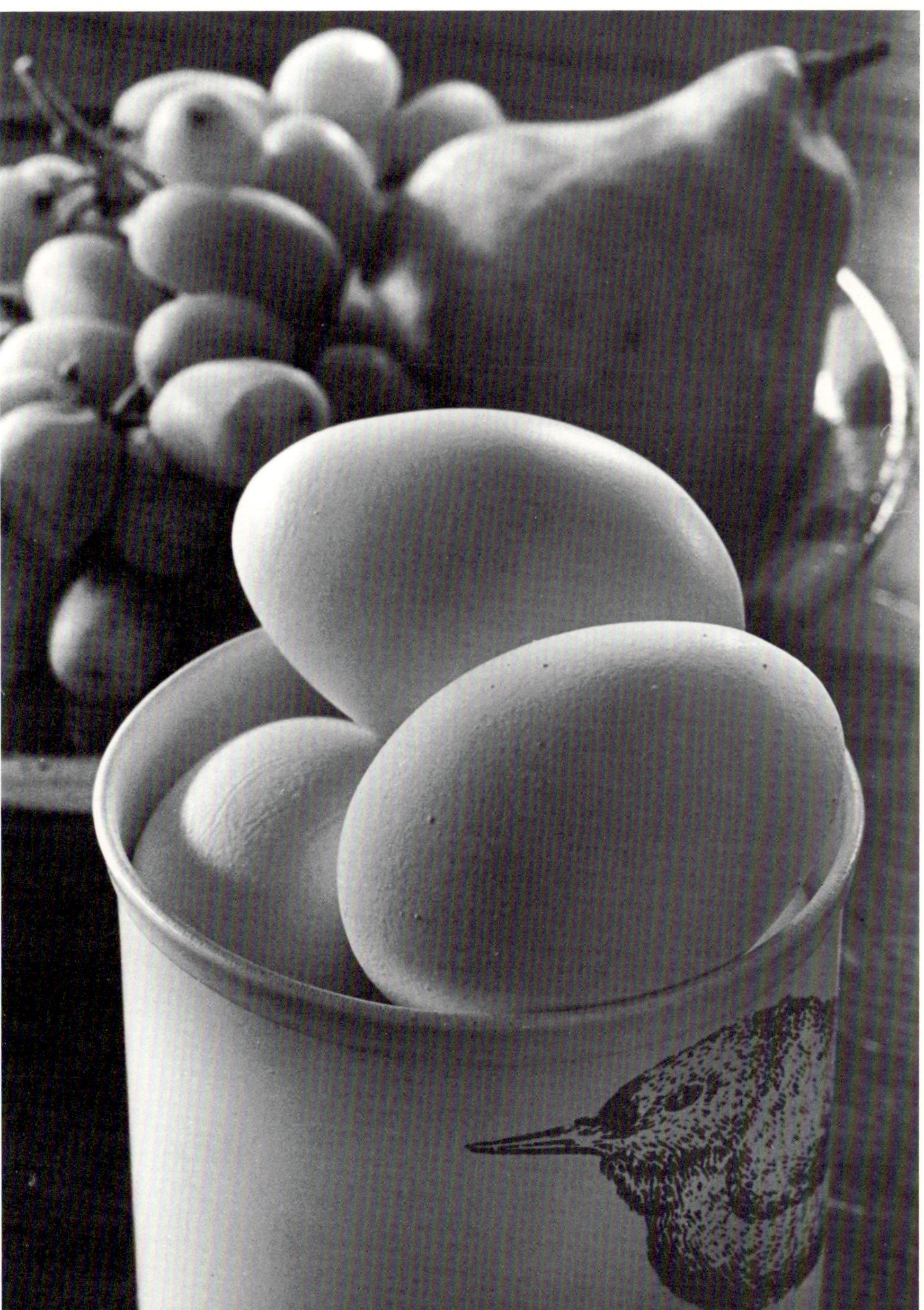

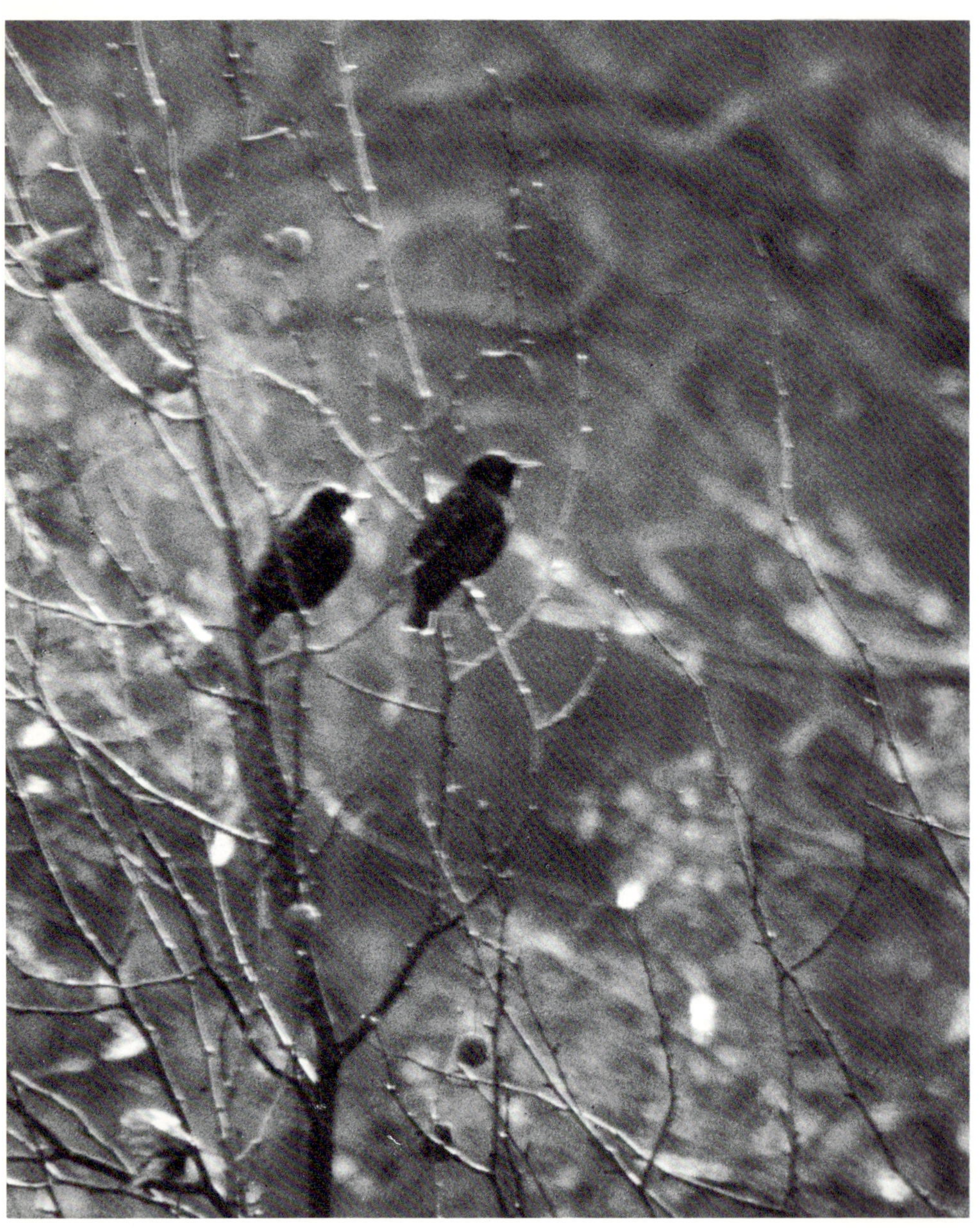

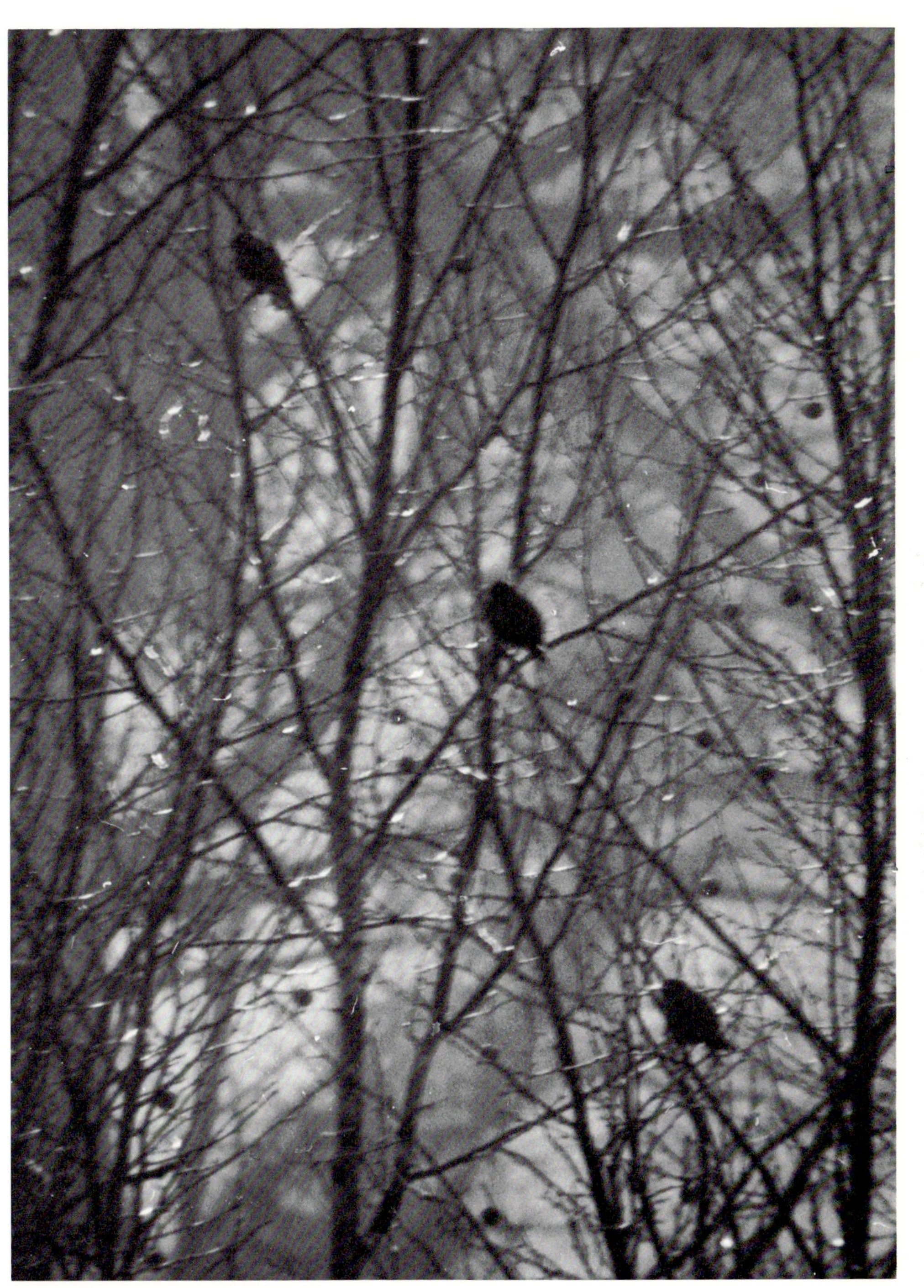

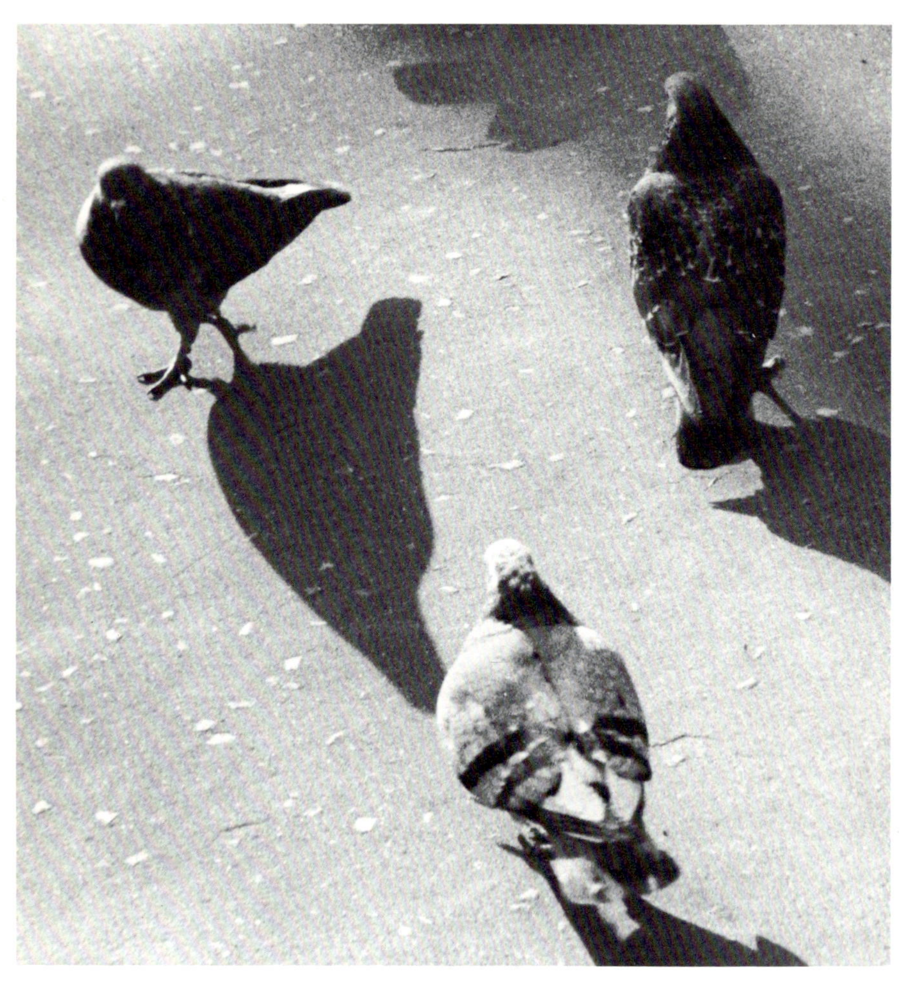

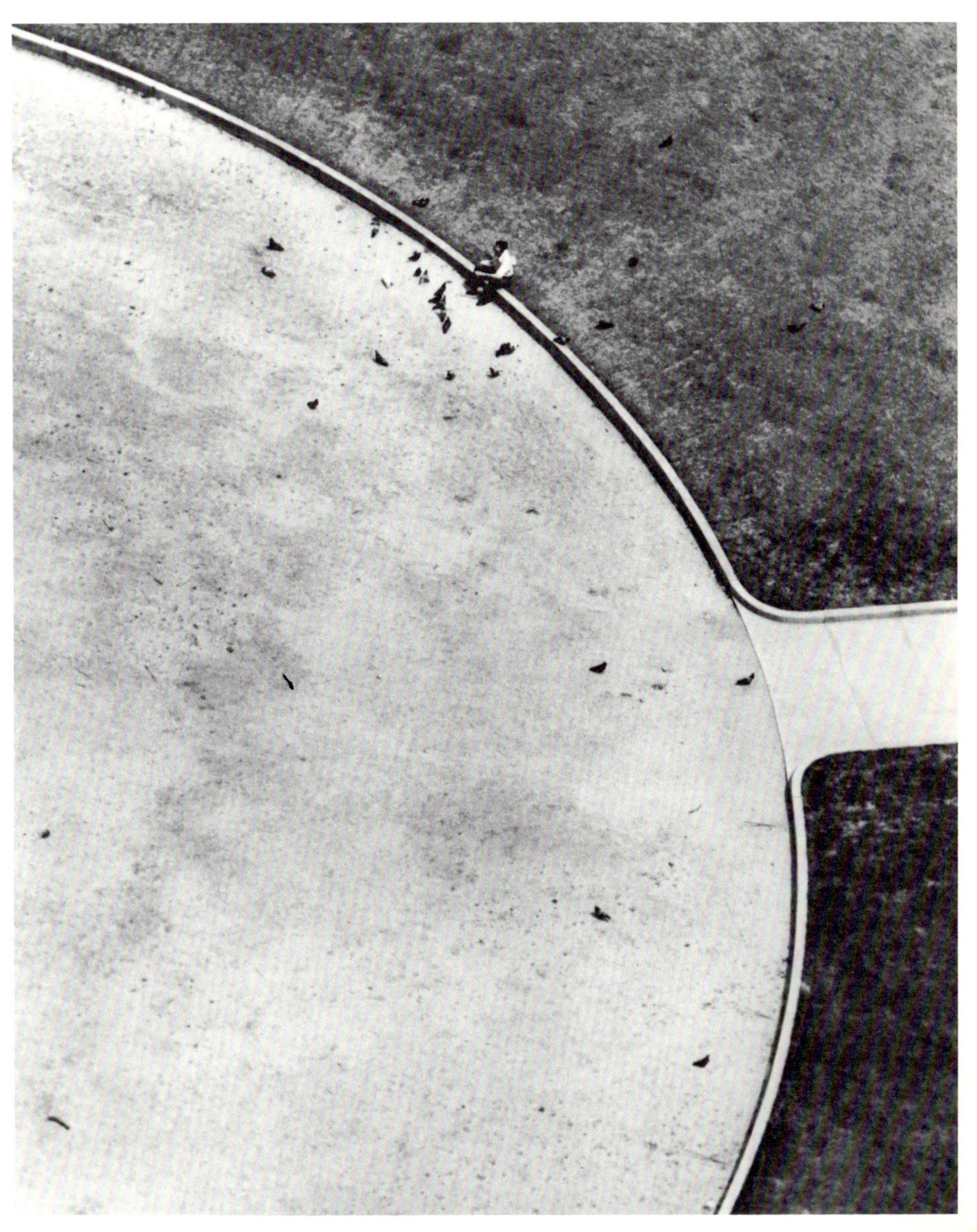

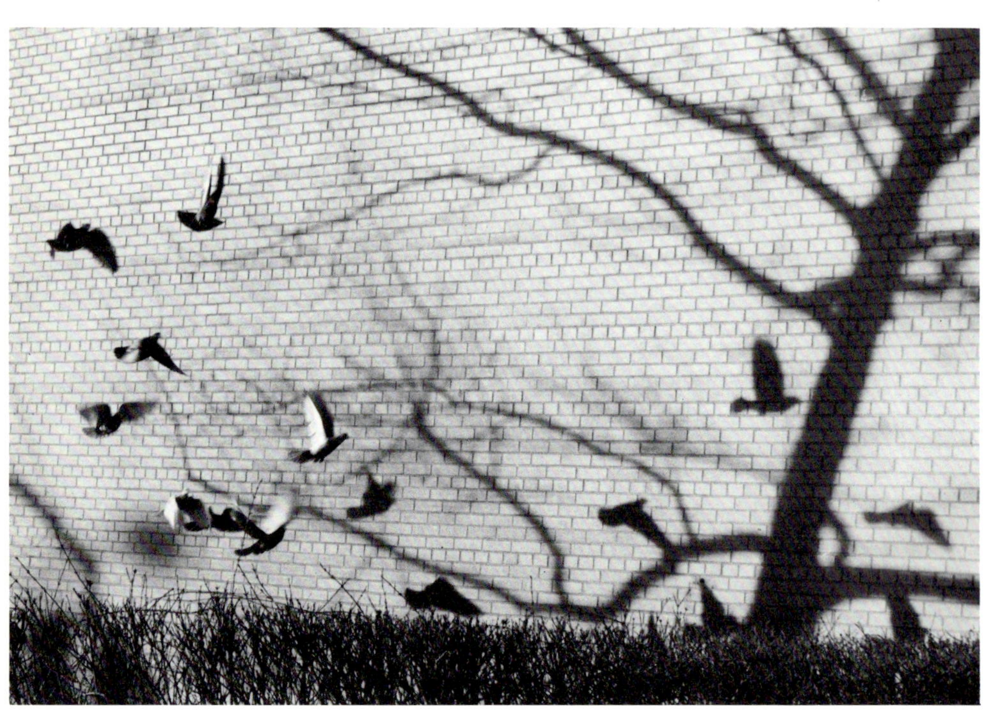

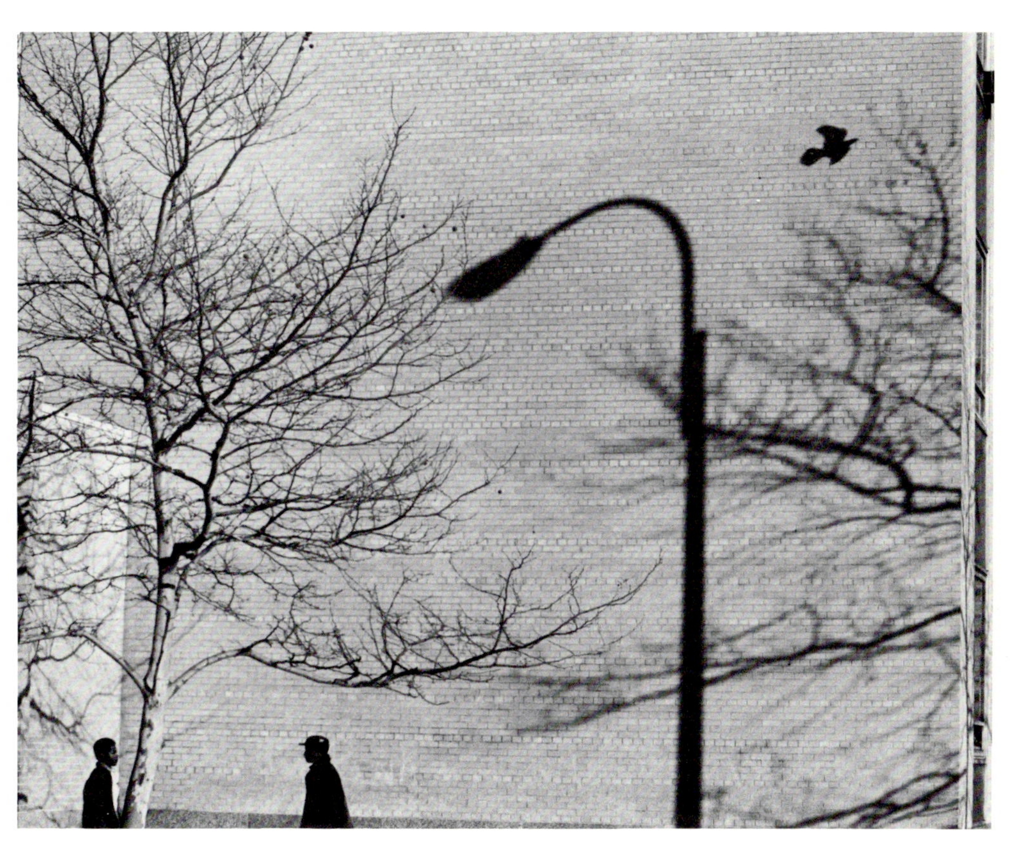

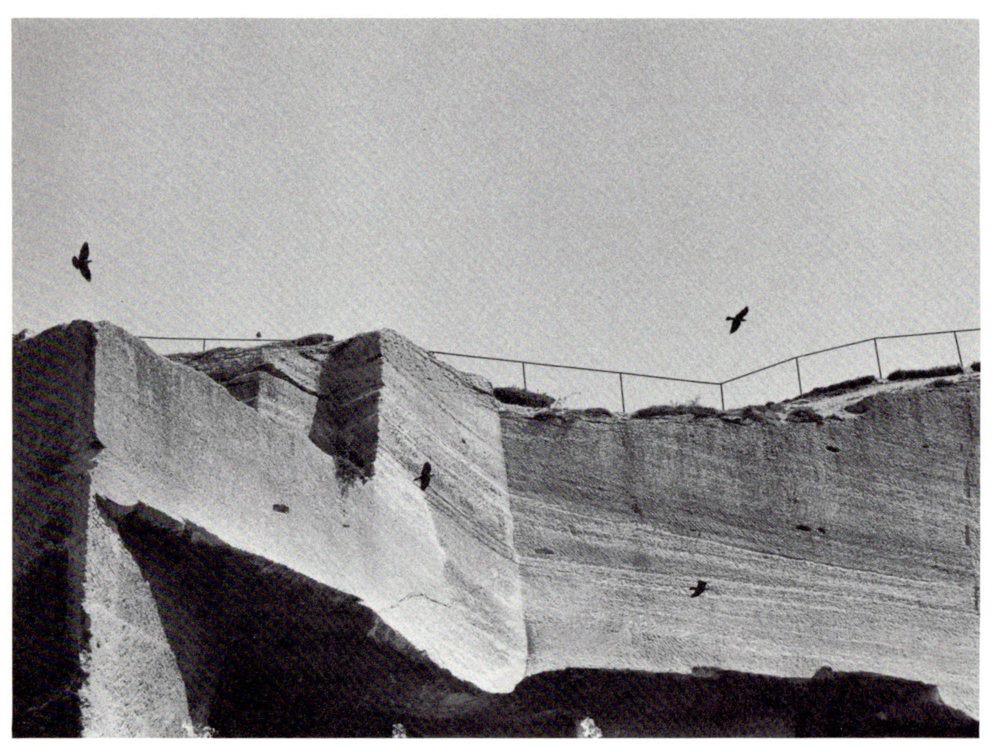

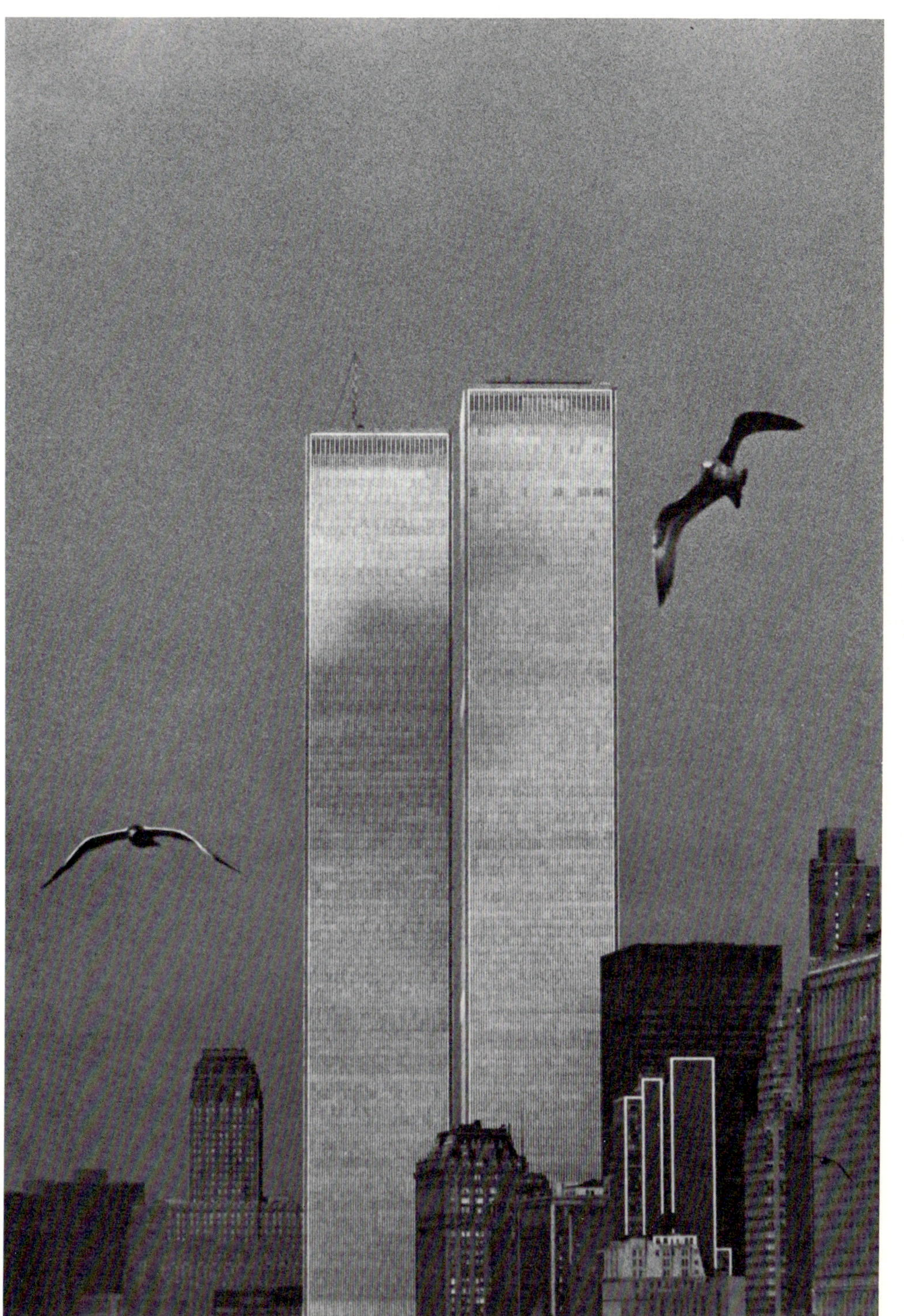

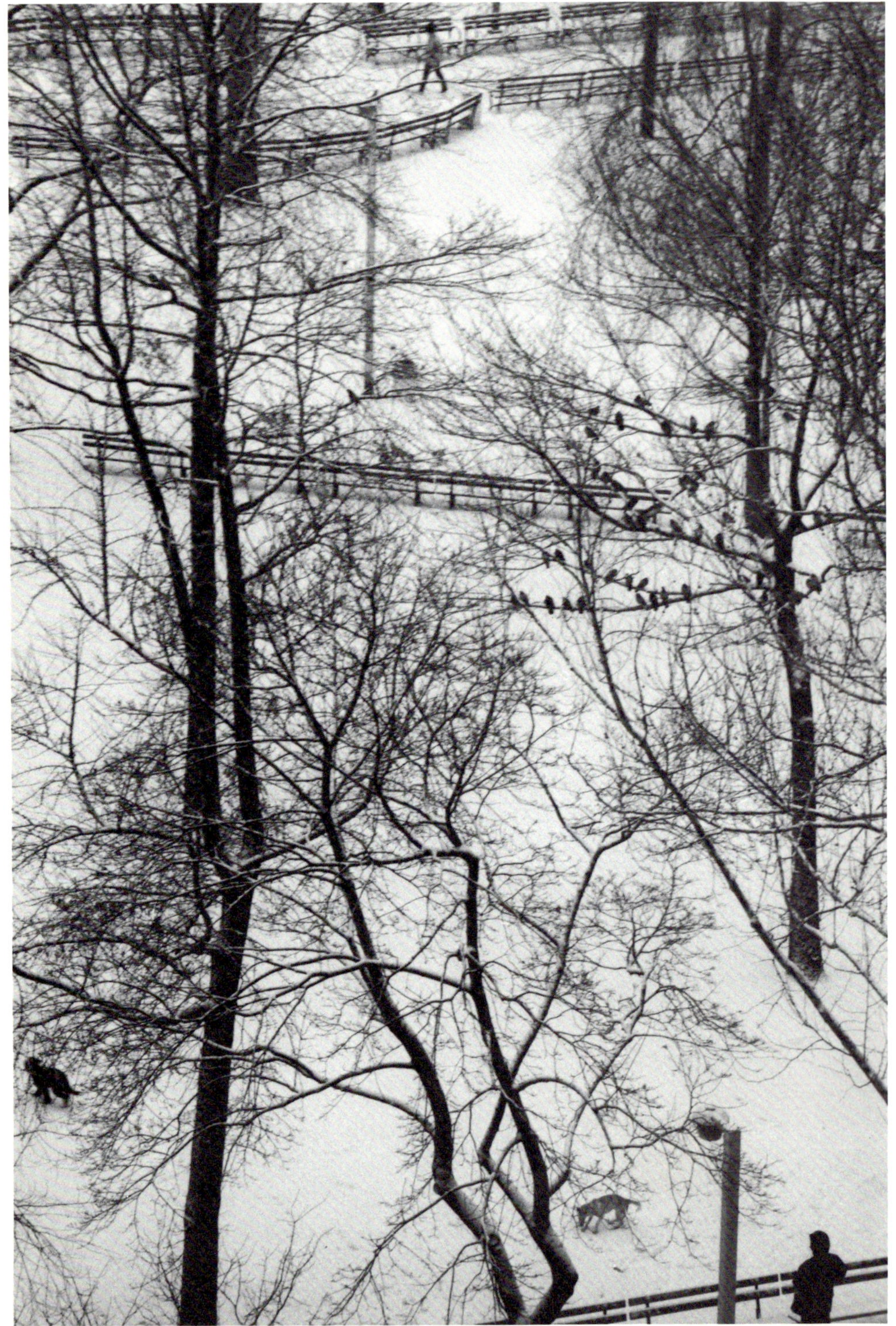

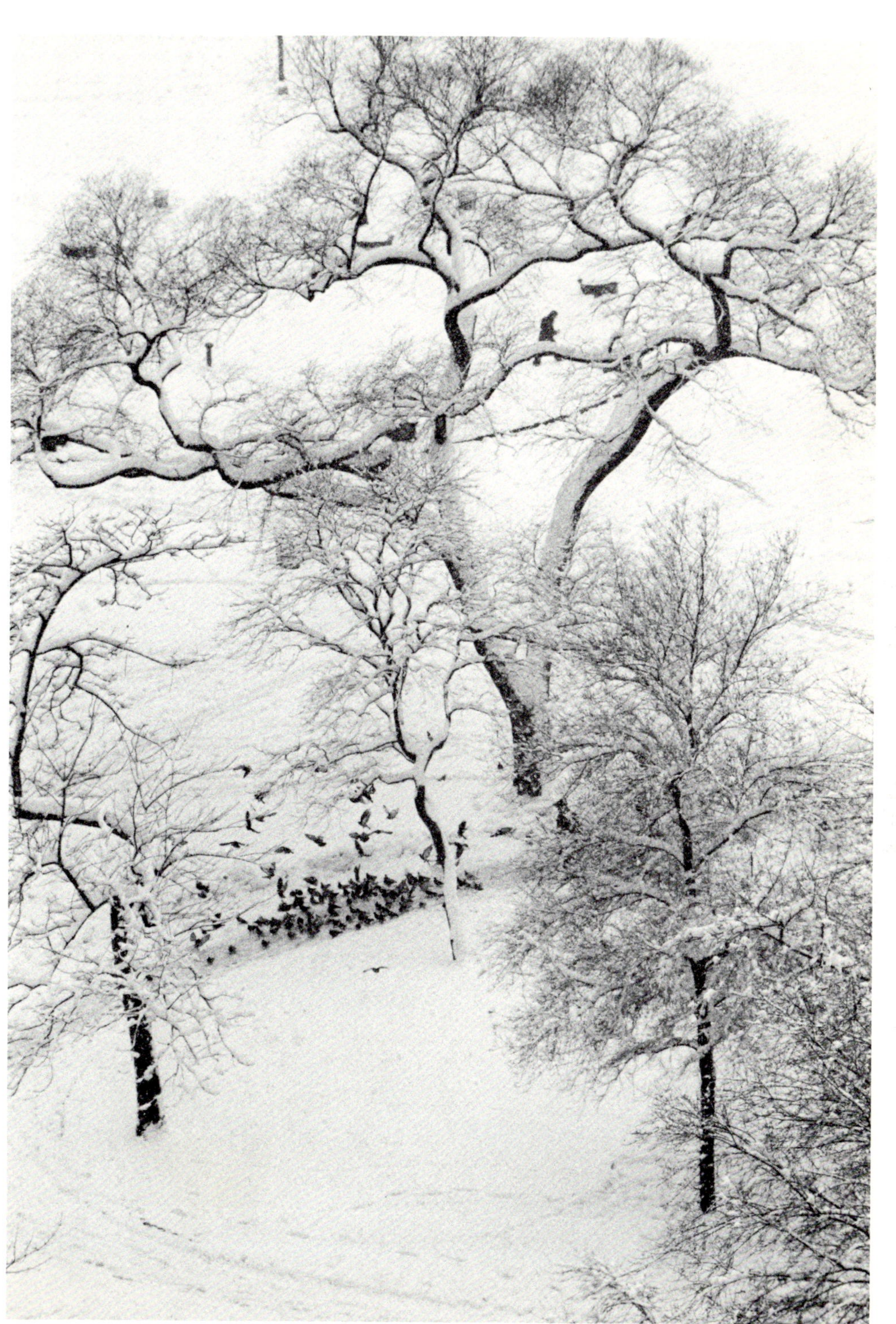

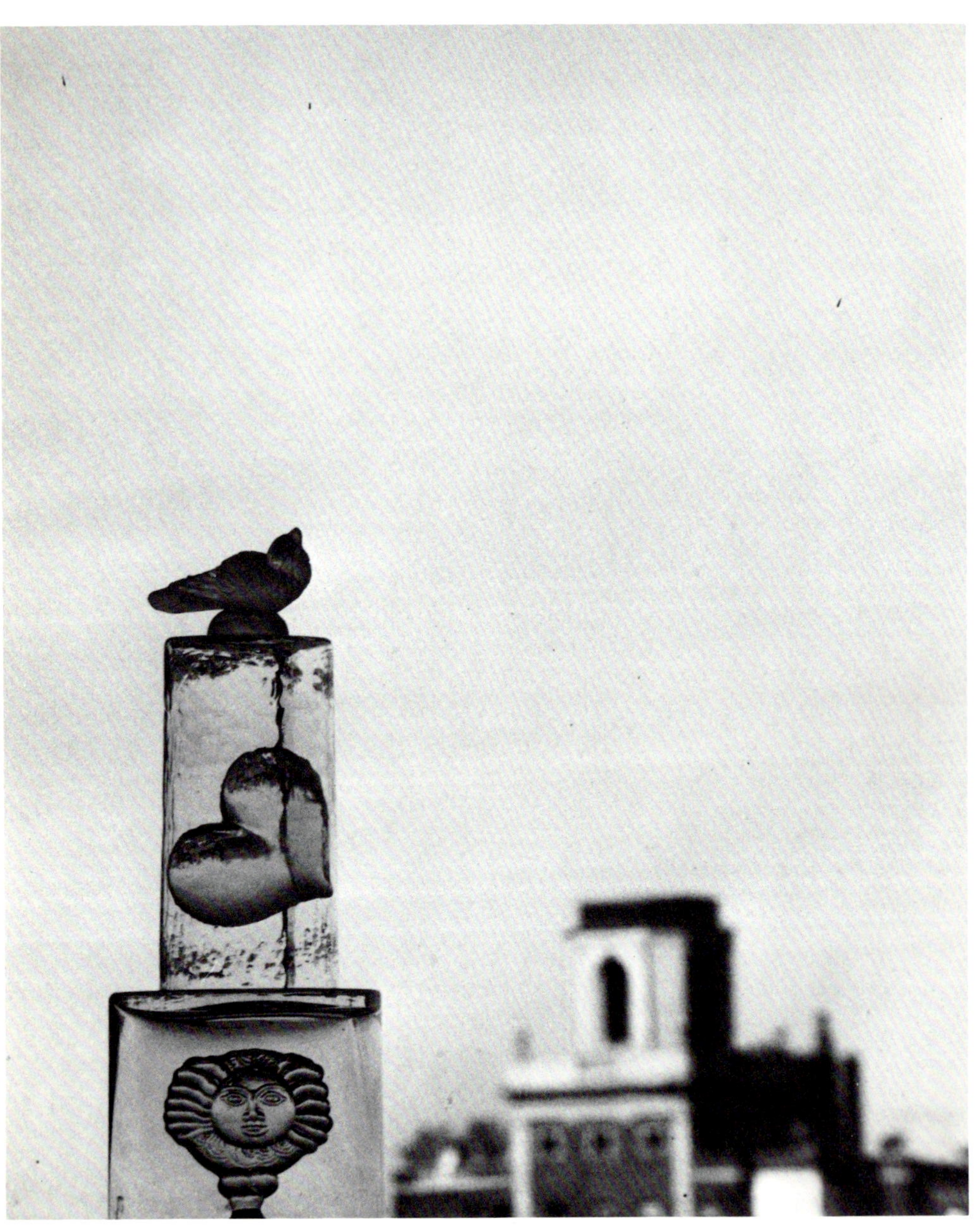

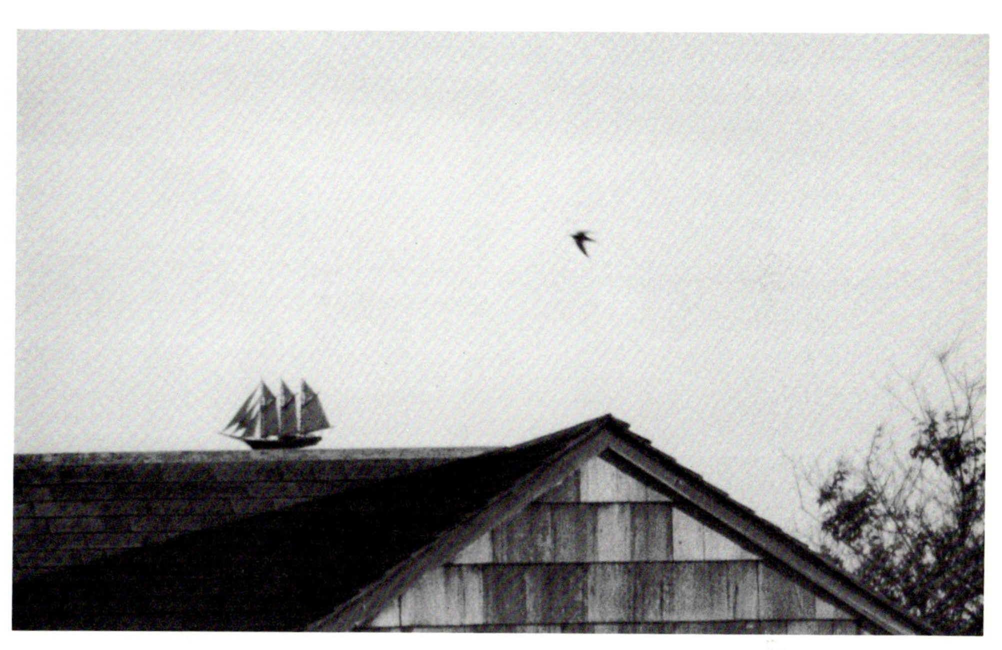

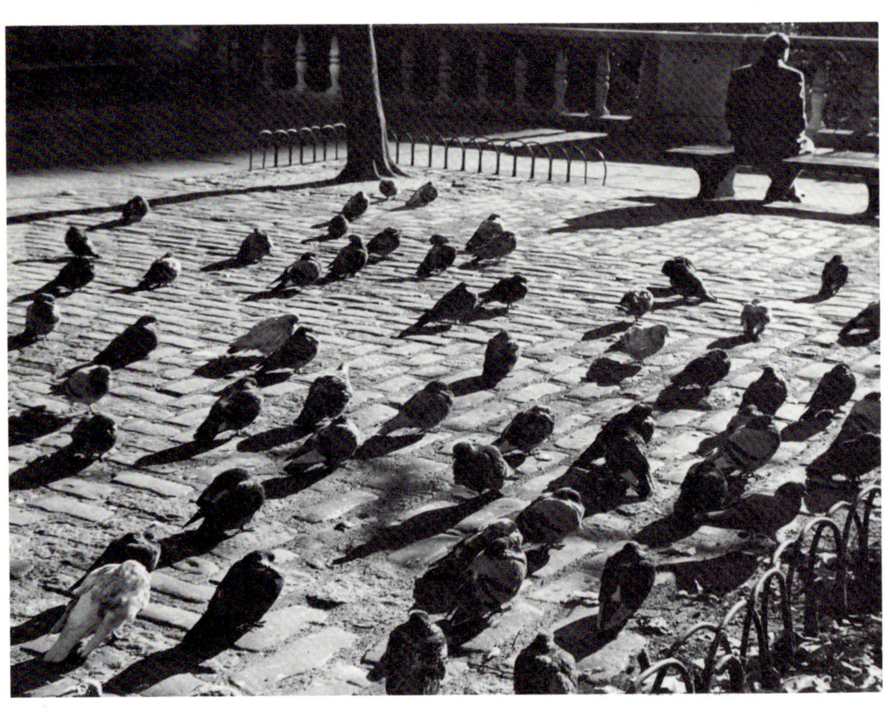

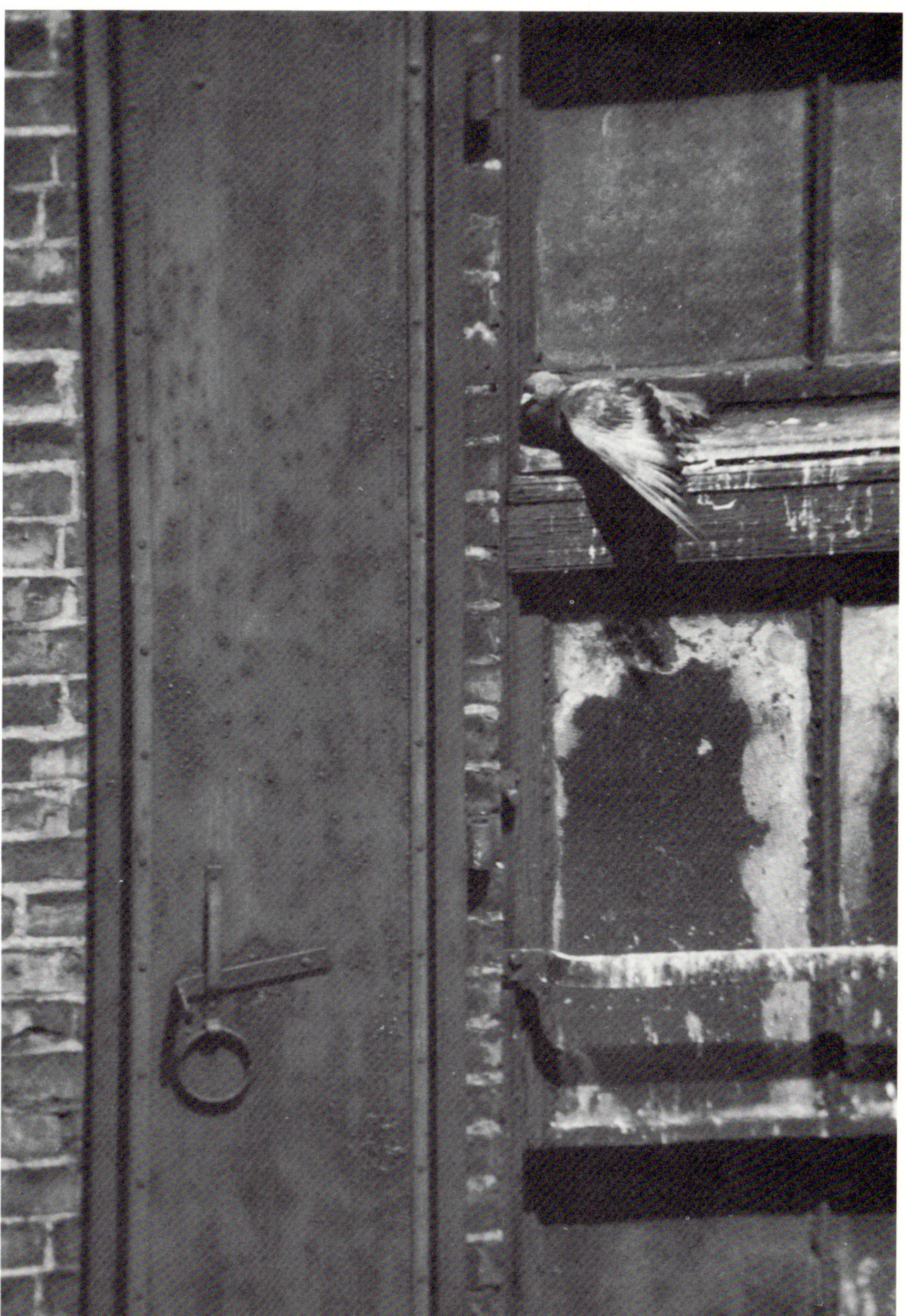

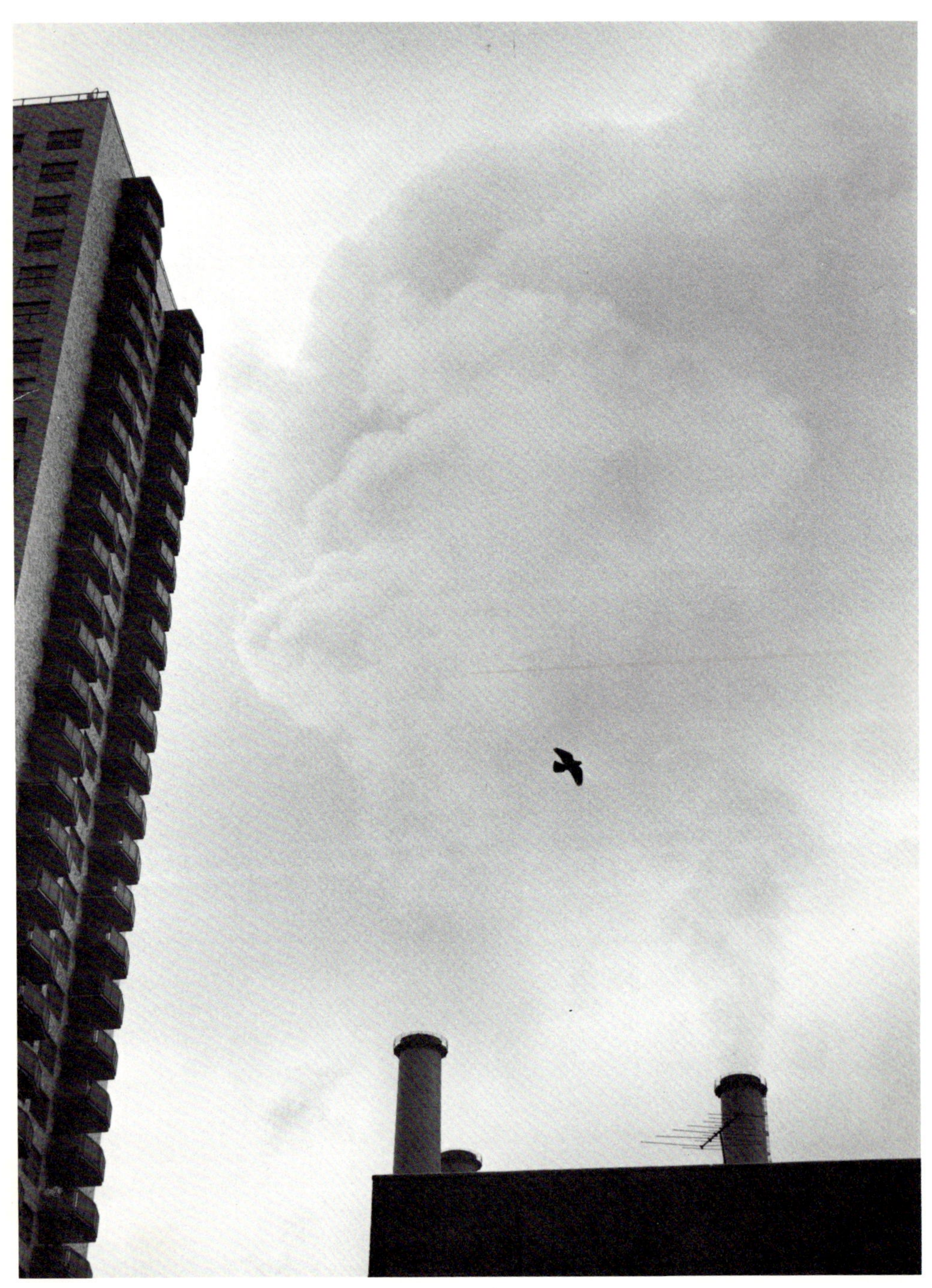

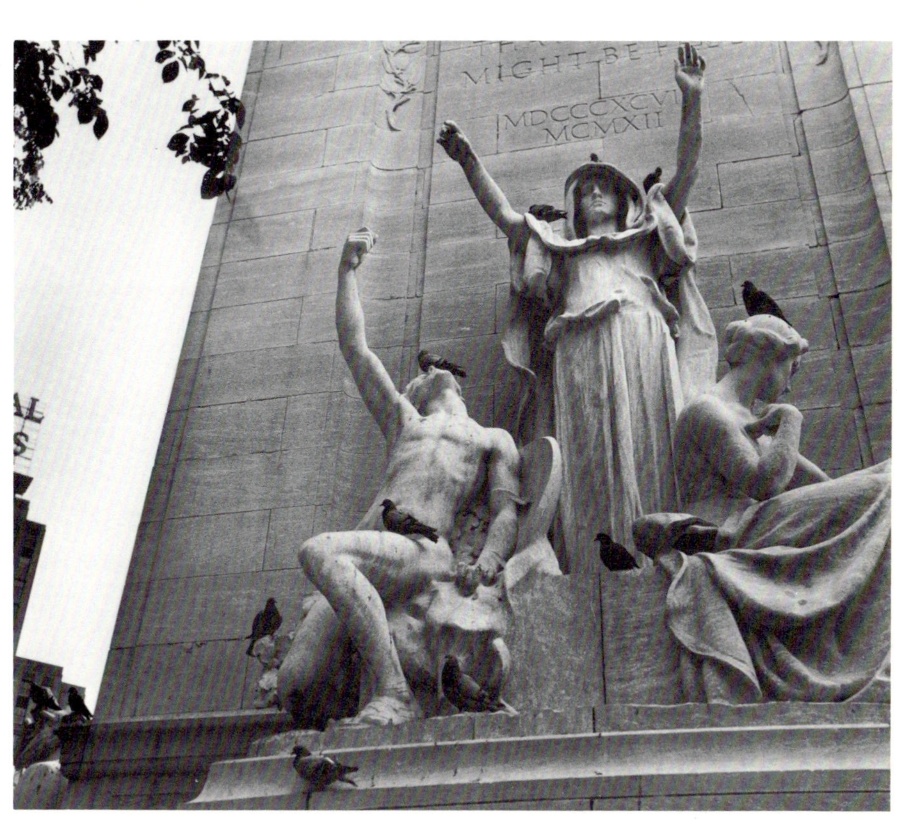
MIGHT BE
MCMXII

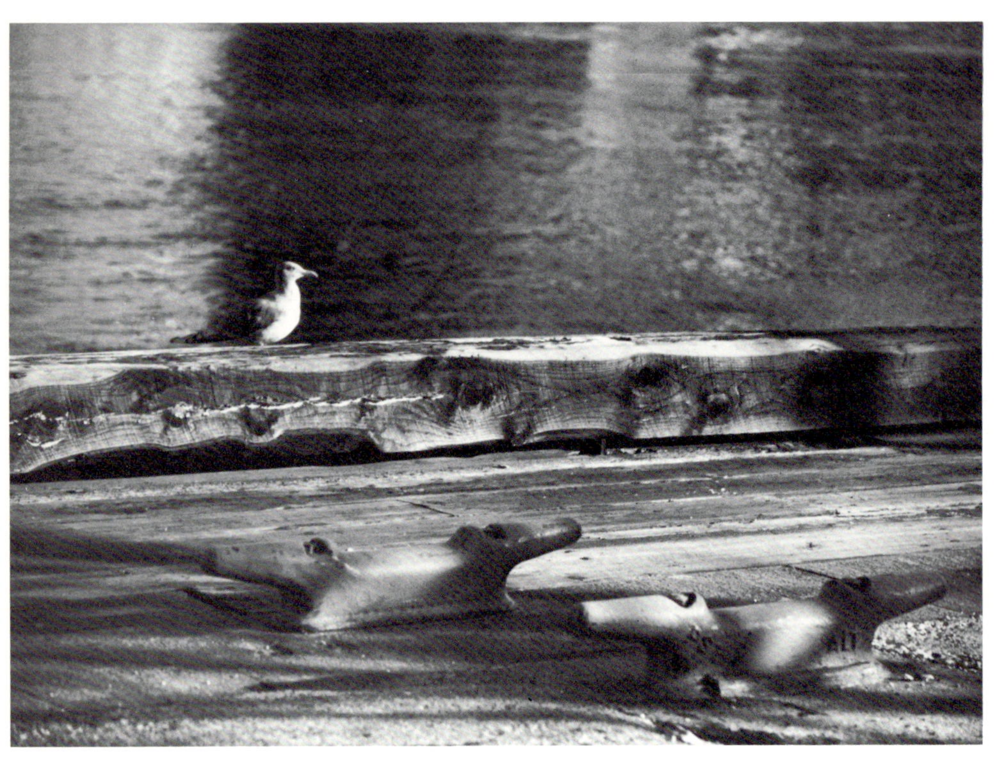

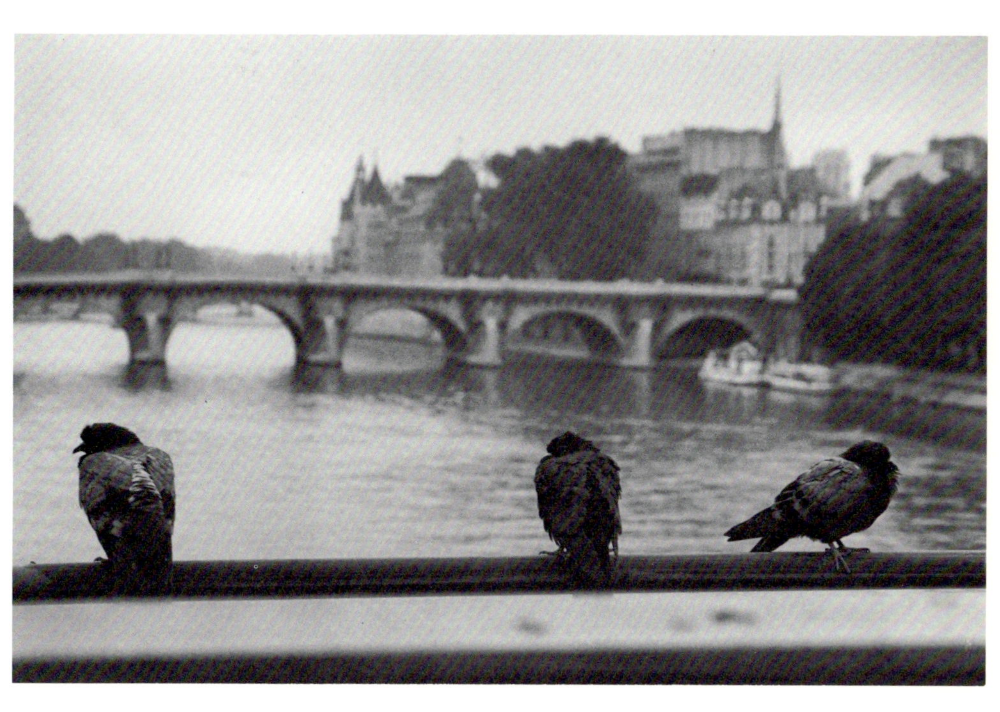

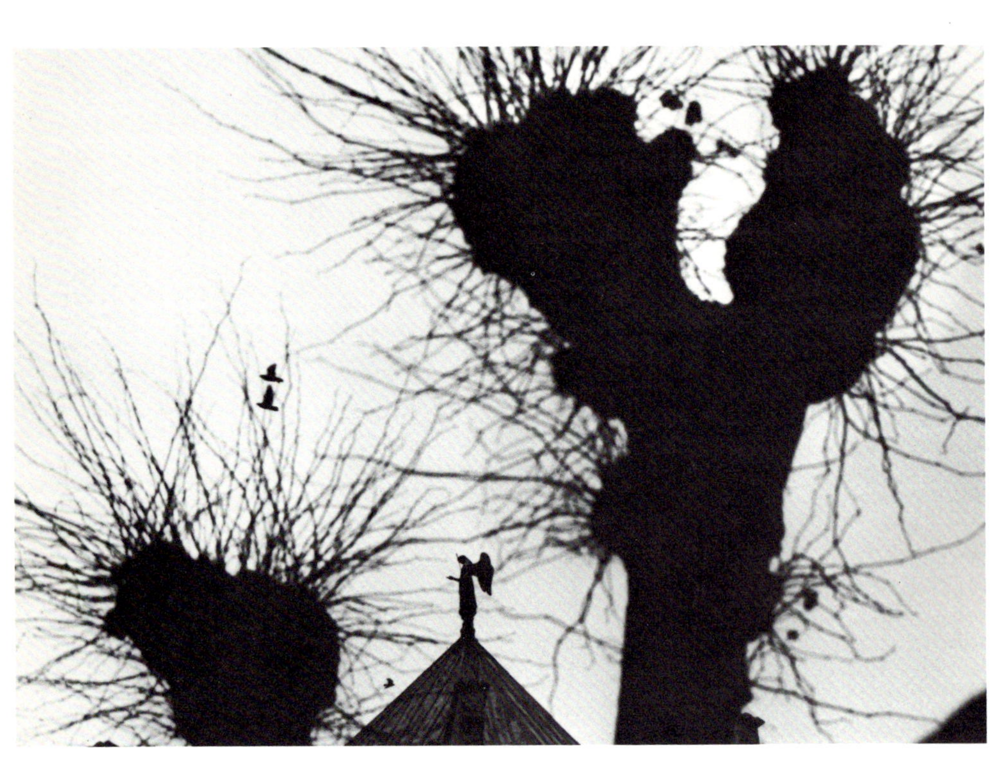

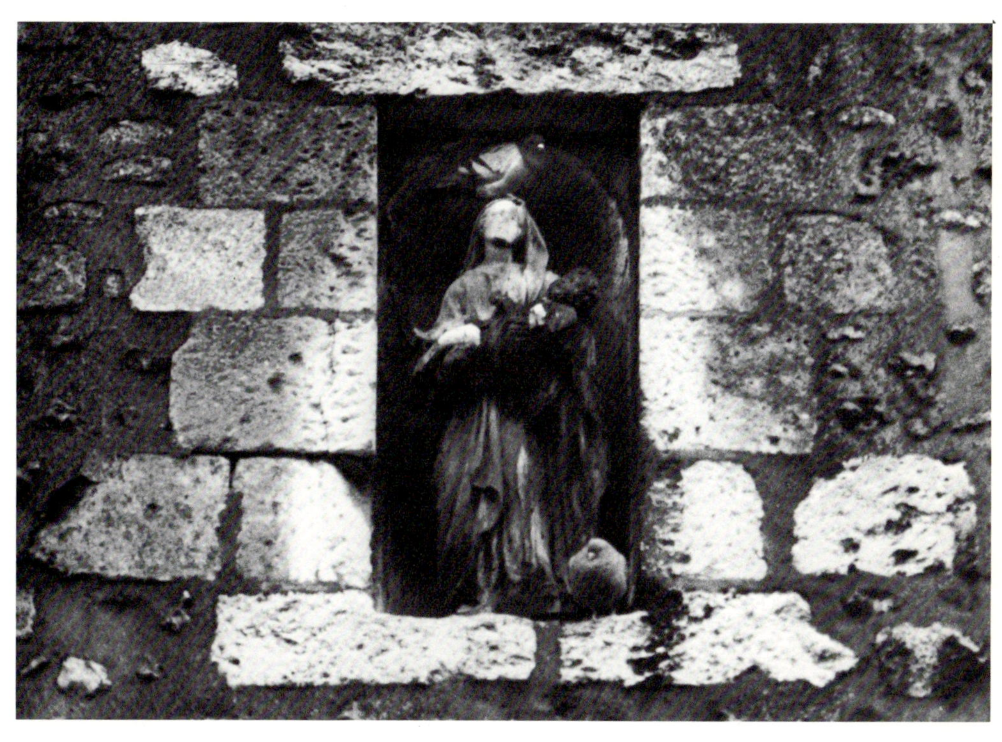

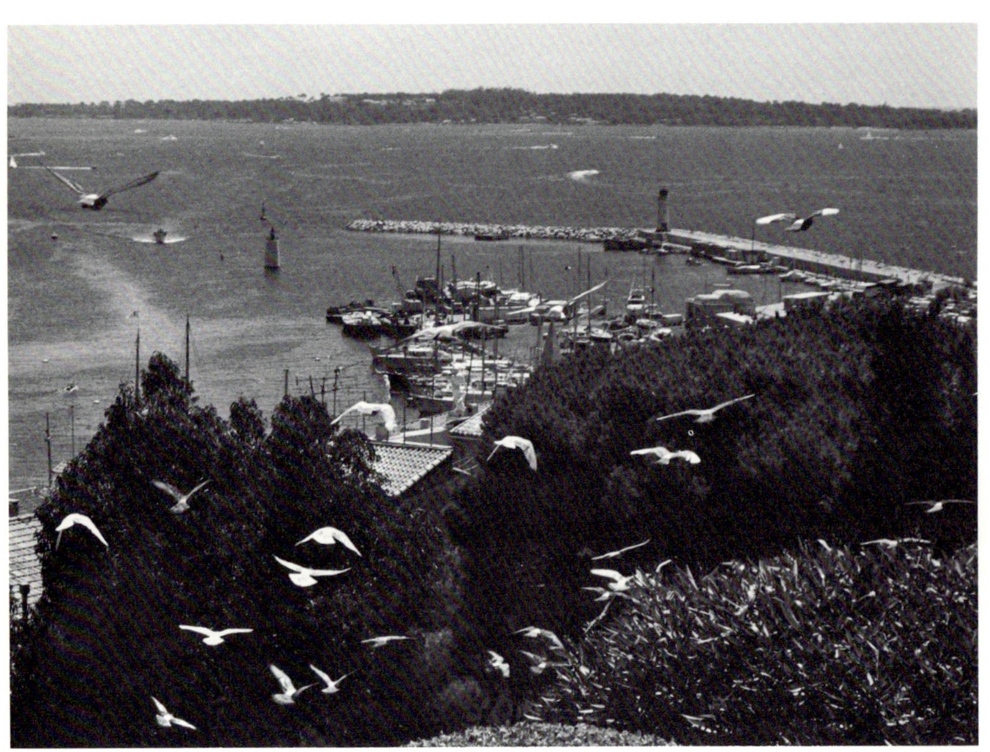

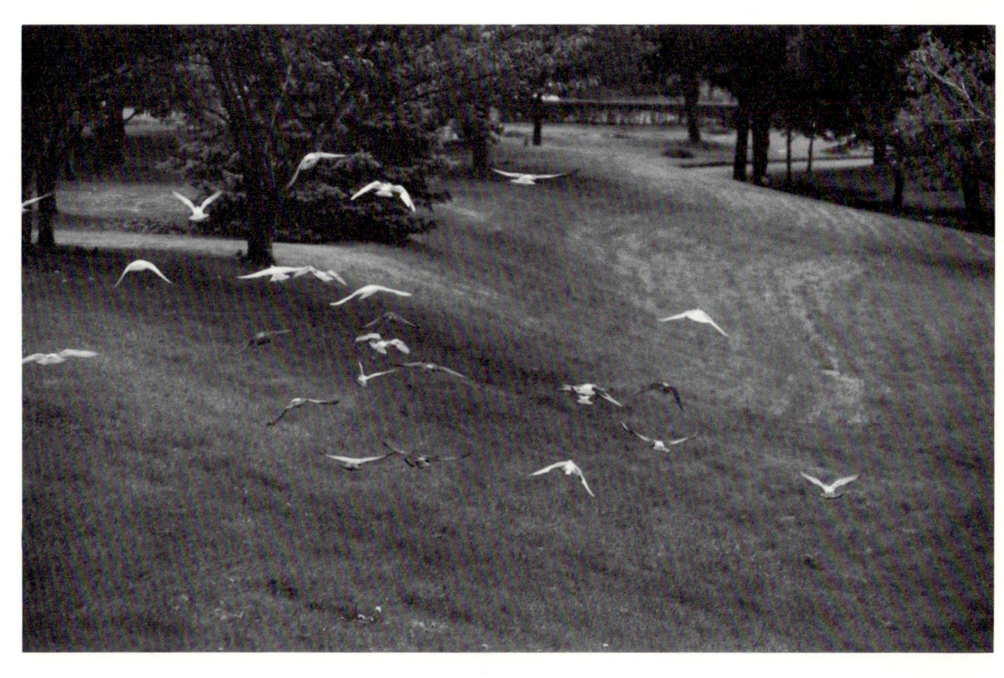

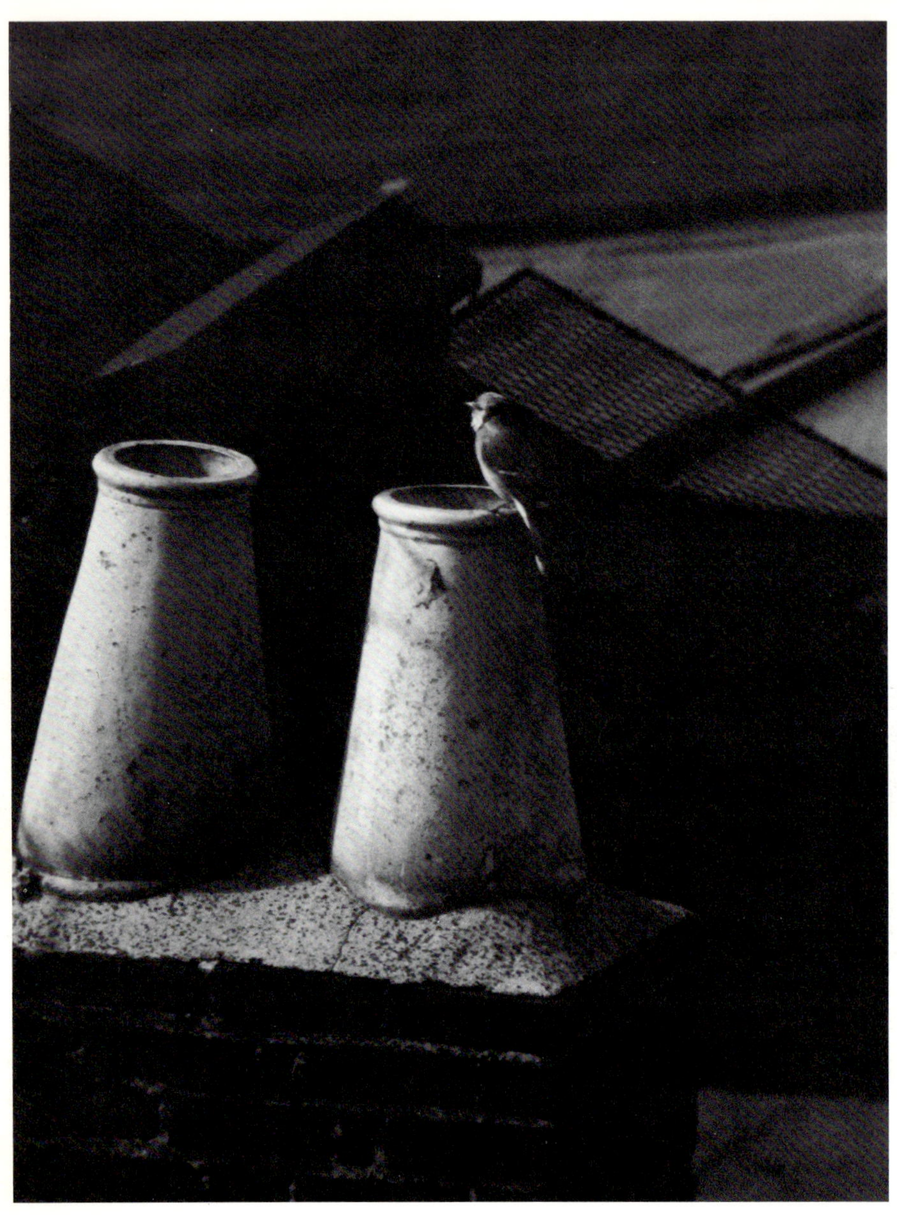

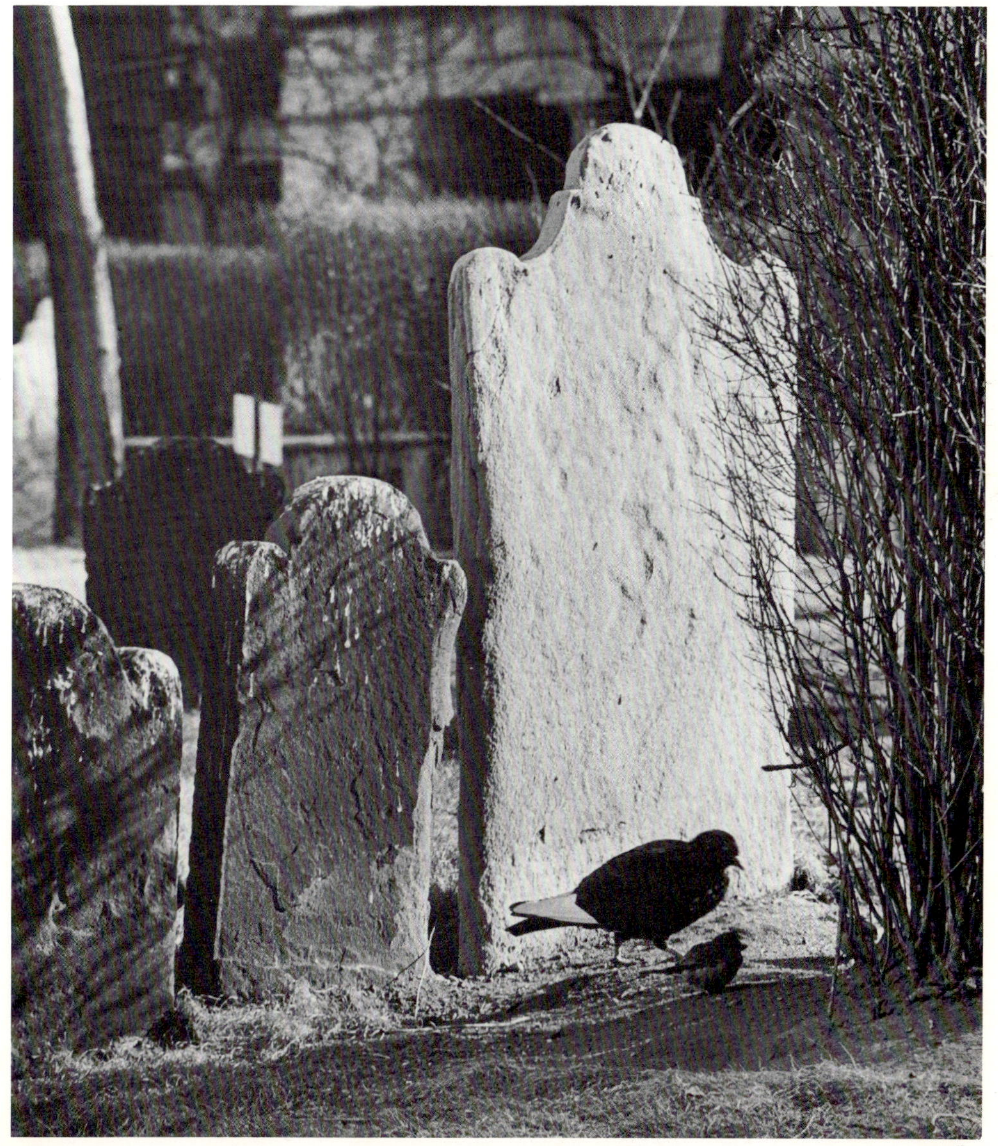

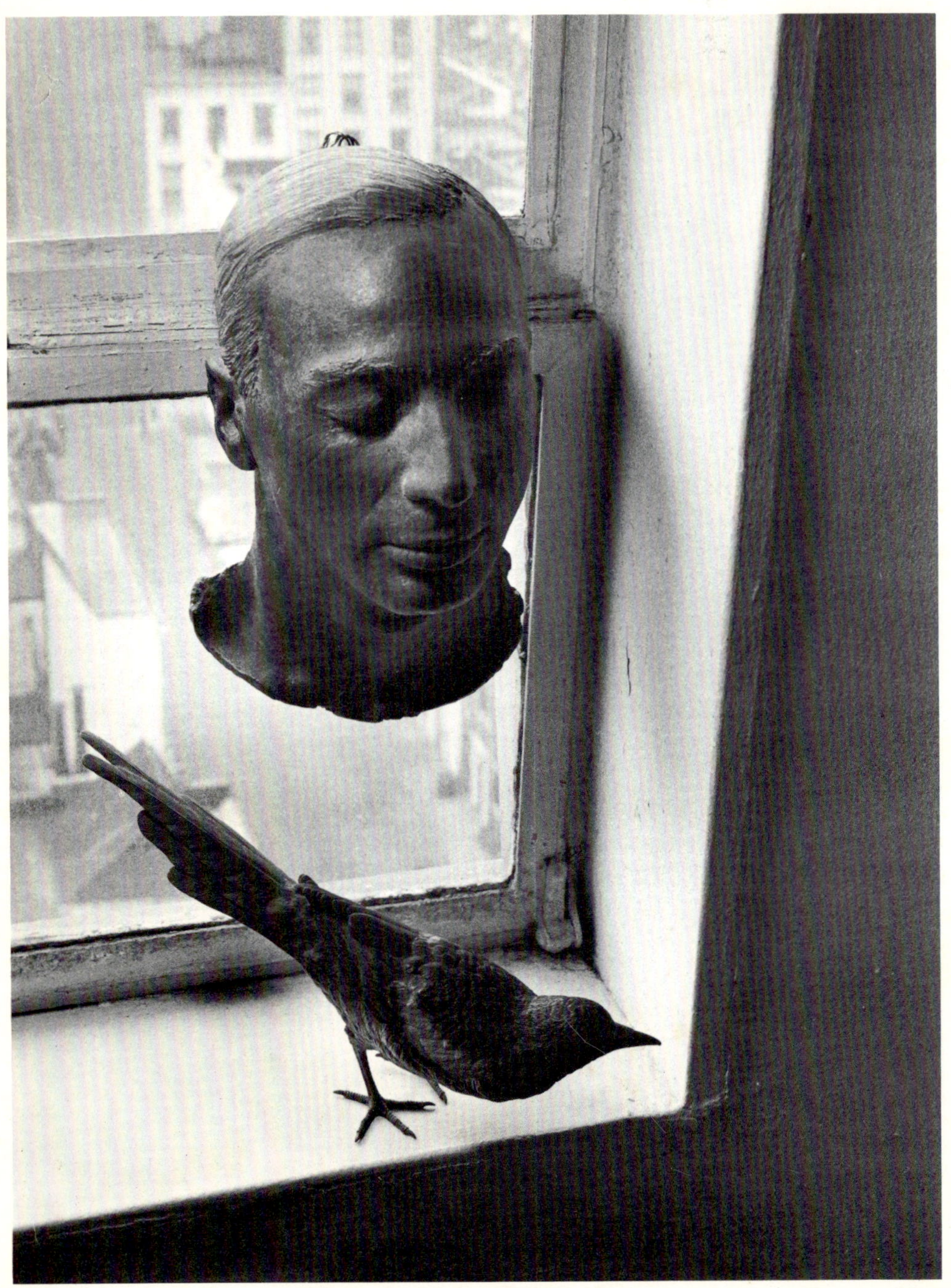